D1084020

THE ESSENTIAL SHAKESPEARE

LONDON
Cambridge University Press
FETTER LANE

NEW YORK · TORONTO
BOMBAY · CALCUTTA · MADRAS
Macmillan

TOKYO
Maruzen Company Ltd

THE GRAFTON PORTRAIT

The Essential Shakespeare

A BIOGRAPHICAL
ADVENTURE

by

J. DOVER WILSON

Our stability is but balance, and wisdom lies
In masterful administration of the unforeseen.
BRIDGES.

Shakespeare led a life of Allegory: his works
are the comments on it. KEATS.

CAMBRIDGE
AT THE UNIVERSITY PRESS
1933

First Edition   *April* 1932
Reprinted   *July* 1932
,,   *Jan.* 1933

PRINTED IN GREAT BRITAIN BY W. LEWIS, M.A.,
AT THE UNIVERSITY PRESS, CAMBRIDGE

CONTENTS

Note. The frontispiece is reproduced, by permission of the John Rylands Librarian, from a portrait of an unknown man, Shakespeare's exact contemporary. It was first discovered in 1907, at Winston-on-Tees, near Darlington and now hangs in the Rylands Library, Manchester; it is known as the "Grafton Portrait" because it originally came from Grafton Regis, Northamptonshire.

PREFACE

I HAVE to thank the Council of the British Academy for its kind permission to reprint one or two brief passages from a lecture I delivered before that body in 1929, entitled *The Elizabethan Shakespeare*.

In a book of this scope and size it would be absurd to attempt a record of my indebtedness to previous writers: let it suffice to say that my creditors are more than I can number and the liability beyond my discharge. But two names I must mention. I had hoped to break a lance with an old friend of Cambridge days, Lytton Strachey, in the last chapter, which was first written as a reply to his brilliant essay, *Shakespeare's Final Period*. But just as I was going to press, he laid his pen aside to join "the loveliest and the best", and I have removed all traces of disagreement except one nameless reference.

I could wish to associate the last chapter too with the name of Sir Edmund Chambers. Though of course the book as a whole owes more than I can estimate to his *William Shakespeare: a study of facts and problems*, I admit to my shame that it was not until it was all but complete, and my theory of *The Tempest* and of what he calls Shakespeare's "conversion" had been worked out, that I read his early prefaces, recently reprinted as *Shakespeare: a survey*. It was interesting to discover that in respect to the last phase we were on somewhat the same tack, and though I differ with him sharply on certain important details, as he no doubt will with me, I derive much encouragement from our measure of agreement.

I hope my title will not be misunderstood. "Here, in a nutshell, is the kind of man I believe Shakespeare to have been", is what it is intended to convey. I might perhaps have called it "A credible Shakespeare".

J. D. W.

February, 1932

WHAT IS A POET?

He is a man speaking to men: a man, it is true, endued with more lively sensibility, more enthusiasm and tenderness, who has a greater knowledge of human nature, and a more comprehensive soul, than are supposed to be common among mankind; a man pleased with his own passions and volitions, and who rejoices more than other men in the spirit of life that is in him; delighting to contemplate similar volitions and passions as manifested in the goings-on of the Universe, and habitually impelled to create them where he does not find them.

WORDSWORTH

I

IMAGES OF SHAKESPEARE

Look here upon this picture and on this
Hamlet.

THIS LITTLE BOOK attempts, as many hundreds before it have attempted, to interpret the career of William Shakespeare, poet and dramatist for all time, and principal entertainer of Elizabethan and Jacobean London. And if I am asked what excuse I offer for adding even one more pebble to the enormous cairn of commentary and biography beneath which the real Shakespeare somewhere lies, I can only reply that I heartily dislike some of the current interpretations which pass as orthodox, and have long wished to work out another which might seem more in accord at once with common sense and with what we know of the life and spirit of other poets and creative artists.

My own interpretation is of course influenced by personal prepossessions, as all general notions of Shakespeare must be, but I can at least claim that it is no piece of preconceived sentimentalism. Rather, it has revealed itself bit by bit through a study of the plays, of the period and of the known facts of the life, a study carried on continuously for over thirty years and culminating during the last ten of them in the most intimate relationship which anyone, not an actor and dramatist of genius like Mr Granville Barker, can now have with Shakespeare; I mean the editing of his works from the originals. It is true

that the edition I am concerned with has so far em-
braced the Comedies only, but this in some degree
puts me at an advantage, since it means at any rate
that I start at the right end, the Elizabethan end;
most previous biographers, to my thinking, having
gone astray by considering Shakespeare too much
from the standpoint of his later work, written during
the reign of James I.

The sublimity of his subject, and the comparative
poverty of contemporary information about it, expose anyone who undertakes to write a life of
Shakespeare to many perils, but the greatest of
them all is the personal equation. It is indeed impossible that he should altogether escape it; for he
must begin by framing some general conception of
what he takes to be Shakespeare's spirit and personality, which is as if a blind man who could not
climb should try to form a general idea of the
Matterhorn or Mont Blanc from every point of
view and in all weather conditions. Yet he may
observe two precautions which will go some way
towards saving him from absolute disaster. In the
first place he should make all possible and legitimate
use of the lives of other poets and artists to throw
light upon the life of Shakespeare, acquainting himself as well with what other poets and artists have
thought about their greatest fellow, since such
thoughts will be of infinitely more value than anything he could excogitate out of his own feeble
imagination. And secondly he should do what in
him lies to make clear both to himself and to his
readers what personal prepossessions about Shake-

speare he starts with. Every biographer has them, though few confess them, and most are unconscious of them. I observe that even Sir Edmund Chambers, who appears in his *William Shakespeare: a study of facts and problems* as an arch-sceptic and a sardonic anti-romantic, when composing his earlier book, *Shakespeare: a survey*, followed Sidney's precept "Look in thy heart and write" and found an image there, which is certainly not lacking in romance.

I shall disclose my own image of Shakespeare towards the end of this chapter. At the moment I would insist that this secret image of the heart, of which the biographer may be completely unaware, is too often the root cause of his aberration. What may be called the scientific school of Shakespearian biography furnishes an excellent example. Setting the plays and poems aside as "impersonal" and therefore of no value whatever as evidence, they proceed to build up every available scrap of external information into their structure, without realising that the significance they attach to each scrap depends upon their own implicit conception of the poet, and that the scraps can only be held together by a plentiful supply of mortar in the form of suppressed hypothesis. The best known writer of the school is Sidney Lee, whose magisterial *Life of William Shakespeare* is the standard authority upon the subject. An indispensable reference book of facts, which I shall not hesitate to make use of in the following pages, it offers reading encouraging to the industrious apprentice and flattering to the

3

successful business man; for its theme is the story of the butcher-boy of Stratford who made a fortune in London, and the conclusion it draws is that "his literary attainments and successes were chiefly valued as serving the prosaic end of making a permanent provision for himself and his daughters"; which is like saying that Keats wrote the *Ode to a Nightingale* in order to have something in his stocking against a rainy day with Fanny Brawne. Such writers are dangerous because their show of objectivity and science may conceal their premises from the very elect. The image in Lee's heart was that of a typical English manufacturer who happened to deal in *Twelfth Nights* and *Lears* instead of brass tacks. Now Lee himself was not in the least like this. Where then did his image come from? An unimaginative man, he was not likely to have invented it. As we shall see in Chapter III, he got it partly from an earlier biographer, Halliwell-Phillipps; but he also paid frequent visits to Stratford, and there he had ample opportunities of gazing at a false image which would suggest all the ideas he required. In a word, the *Life* that Lee gave us was not the life of William Shakespeare the man and the poet, but the life that 'William Shakespeare', the bust in Stratford Church, might have lived had he ever existed in flesh and blood.

The Stratford bust is the only portrait of the poet which can claim any sort of authority, seeing that the Droeshout frontispiece to the First Folio is nothing but a clumsy engraving derived from it, and that all other portraits are themselves derived from either the bust or the engraving. Moreover the monument was erected at Stratford shortly after Shakespeare's death, before 1623 at any rate, and it is generally supposed that the features were modelled directly from a mask taken from Shakespeare's face, alive or dead. Yet, despite everything, I make bold to say that this bust is one of the greatest of all obstacles to the true understanding of Shakespeare. Here are a few descriptive notes of it from a learned essay by Mr M. H. Spielmann, which is objective but by no means hostile in spirit: "its wooden appearance and vapid expression", "its coarsely-shaped, half-moon eyebrows, more like George Robey's than anybody else's", its staring eyes set "too close together" and like the nose "too small for the face". The essay also draws attention to the extraordinary upper lip, the hanging lower lip, and the general air of stupid and self-complacent prosperity. All this might suit well enough with an affluent and retired butcher, but does gross wrong to the dead poet. "Some men there are love not a gaping pig", and for half the unlearned world this Shakespeare simply will not do. The Stratford bust, and Lee's *Life* inspired by gazing too much upon it, are together, I am convinced, mainly responsible for the campaign against "the man of Stratford" and the attempts to dethrone him in favour of Lord Bacon, the Earl of Derby, the Earl of Oxford, the Earl of Rutland, or whatever coroneted pretender may be in vogue at the present moment.

Yet the bust is easily explained. It is the old story, only too familiar to friends and relatives of most men wealthy or famous enough to fall a prey to the second-rate portrait-painter. The job was given to an Anglo-Flemish mason of London, one Garratt Janssen, who knew what belonged to a monument and executed the task in a workman-like and (as monuments go) highly creditable fashion. The proportions are admirable, and the architectural design, with its pillars and canopy, its mantled shield, and its twin cherubs, is even beautiful. But one thing was clearly quite beyond the workman's scope —the human face, the face that happened to be Shakespeare's! And if Mistress Shakespeare and the poet's daughters disliked the portrait, what could they do? In cases of this kind, the family of the victim is helpless. There was the monument, complete and no doubt paid for, paid for perhaps by friends as well as relatives. And what a fine monument it was—all but the face! As to that, widow and daughters could only grin, like the travesty that confronted them, and bear it.

But we need not; and it is time an end was put to the scandal of three centuries. For Janssen's self-satisfied pork-butcher and the Folio engraving taken from it, which Mr J. C. Squire has called "the pudding-faced effigy of Droeshout", stand between us and the true Shakespeare, and are so obviously false images of the greatest poet of all time that the world turns from them in disgust and thinks it is turning from Shakespeare himself. A banner of the crusade against Janssen and Droeshout is hoisted in the frontispiece to this book. It is a reproduction of a beautiful portrait, now hanging in the Rylands

Library at Manchester, of a young man of Shakespeare's time. As the inscription at the top shows, he was Shakespeare's exact contemporary, and a comparison with the Droeshout engraving reveals the further coincidence that the relative distances from the chin to the lower lip, from the lower lip to the tip of the nose, from the tip of the nose to the lower eyelid, from the lower eyelid to the eyebrow, and from the eyebrow to the top of the forehead, are identical in both portraits, a fact which is not to be despised seeing that honest Droeshout and Janssen would take a pride in getting their faces right "by the squier". The similarity too of the great foreheads is particularly striking. Beyond these coincidences there is nothing whatever to connect the unknown youth of the wonderful eyes and the oval Shelley-like face with the poet who was also twenty-four years old in 1588.

Of course, the picture has been claimed as a genuine Shakespeare portrait. The temptation to do so is almost irresistible; and for my part since I first had it brought to my notice in 1914, the temptation has grown stronger every time I have looked at it. It was encouraging also to learn from his posthumous book published in 1928 that Dr John Smart of Glasgow, the sanest of modern Shakespearian biographers, "found in it his own idea of the youthful Shakespeare and wished it genuine". Yet there is no real evidence, and I do not ask the reader to believe in it or even to wish to believe in it. All I suggest is that he may find it useful in trying to frame his own image of

7

Shakespeare. It will at any rate help him to forget the Stratford bust. Let him take it, if he will, as a painted cloth or arras, drawn in front of that monstrosity, and symbolising the Essential Poet. A portrait of Keats or Shelley would have served the purpose; but since fortune has preserved it for us, this picture of an unknown Elizabethan poet serves better. "I think", wrote Keats humbly, "I shall be among the English poets after my death", and Matthew Arnold cried out upon this "He is; he is with Shakespeare". We are apt to forget at times, in our preoccupation with Shakespeare the Stratford Institution, Shakespeare the National Bard, or even Shakespeare the world-worshipped dramatic interpreter of mankind, that Shakespeare himself is also "among the English poets", is with Keats and with Shelley. If my frontispiece reminds even one reader of this, it will not be altogether impertinent.

It may remind readers of another thing, which is still more often forgotten: Shakespeare was once young. Indeed, he was never old; for he gave up writing at forty-eight and was only fifty-two when he died. Yet for most people he is a kind of Grand Old Man of literature. This is due, partly to the Stratford bust, but chiefly I think to the general trend of Shakespearian criticism since Coleridge, which has concentrated upon the tragedies and later plays like *The Tempest*, and has left the comedies and histories in comparative neglect. Thus we have come to look at Shakespeare through the wrong end of the biographical telescope, to think of him as pre-eminently a tragic poet, facing the vastidity of the universe, wrestling with the problems of evil and disaster—as a man, in short, of brooding temper, of lofty thought, of grave demeanour, and, after passing through the cleansing fires, of cheerful serenity of mind. This Olympian vision might do perhaps for Goethe, who seemed Athene-like to spring into the world in full panoply of philosophic calm, but Shakespeare I am convinced never at any time of his life even remotely resembled it.

The tragic Shakespeare, as we shall see, was a suffering Shakespeare; and the serenity of *The Tempest* was rather the serenity of recovery after sickness, or of peace after a hurricane, than anything aloof or pontifical. Shakespeare was more akin to Dostoieffsky than to Goethe; or perhaps it is better to think of him as a kind of larger and happier Keats who lived on to tread the *via dolorosa* that Dostoieffsky alone of the moderns has trodden after him. For the Keats and the Dostoieffsky within him, were only part-tenants of an all-human spirit, which expressed itself during most of the first half of his dramatic career in comedy without a parallel in the world's literature for gaiety of heart. Thus when Dr A. C. Bradley, after insisting that "Keats was of Shakespeare's tribe", goes on to suggest that "in quality—and I speak of nothing else—the mind of Shakespeare at three-and-twenty may not have been very different", we gratefully subscribe as regards the creator of Romeo, Juliet, King Richard the Second, *Lucrece* and Oberon's fairy-land, while insisting in our turn that the mind

9

which produced Mercutio, *Love's Labour's Lost*, and Bottom possessed qualities of steel-like brilliance and temper, of self-assurance and poise, of a blithe and delighted acceptance of Life in all its manifestations, which we look for in vain in Keats.

By leaving the comic muse out of the picture, the Victorian image of Shakespeare as the sedate Olympian does him much dishonour, for it means robbing him of a good third of his laurels and ignoring the miracle of his spiritual development. The Comedies came first; the Shakespeare of *King Lear* and *The Tempest* grew out of the Shakespeare who gave us Berowne and the Bastard, Juliet's Nurse and Mistress Quickly, the clowns Lance and Lancelot, Sir Toby Belch and Sir John Falstaff, to name only a few of the greatest rout of unseemly, and often indecent, disreputables that ever teemed from a dramatist's brain. And though the Jacobean Shakespeare became more serious than the Elizabethan, he was never, right up to the end, a whit more "respectable". As for the comedies themselves, with all the verve and gusto of their gay indecorum, who that reads them can doubt that they have been cast up on the shores of time by the most impetuous tide of warm-blooded humanity that ever beat through the heart of man? They are immortal, because of their amazing vitality; and their vitality is an indisputable testimony to the enormous satisfaction that went to their making. Shakespeare wrote to please. "The poet", and it is Wordsworth who speaks, "writes under one restriction only, namely the necessity of giving immediate pleasure."

Shakespeare, therefore, wrote to please his audience. But first and foremost and all the time, he wrote to please himself.

One more false image, and I have done with them—the image of the "impersonal" Shakespeare, of a Shakespeare who keeps himself out of his writings, not excepting the *Sonnets*. It is an aspect of the Olympian Shakespeare we have just been considering, and has been made much of by the "scientific" school of biography because it relieves them of the necessity of checking their notions by the evidence of the plays and the poems. After what has just been said, I shall content myself with a few observations on a single point only.

Elizabethan drama was a social institution which performed many functions since taken over by more specialised agencies. Among other things it was, like the modern newspaper, at once the focus and the purveyor of the London gossip of the day. In a word, it was topical. Now Sidney Lee and those who follow him, insist that here Shakespeare differed from his fellow dramatists, that he preserved himself in this as in other respects unspotted from his world. In taking this line they are to some extent reacting from the extravagancies of F. G. Fleay, who seems to have found little except topicality in Shakespeare's plays. Yet they err as far on one side as he did on the other. Hamlet tells us, and in this Shakespeare is surely for once at any rate speaking through the lips of a character, that "the purpose of playing", which of course includes the purpose of the dramatist, "is, as 'twere to hold the mirror up to nature, to show virtue her own feature, scorn her own image, and the very age and body of the time his form and pressure". That is the gist of the matter, both then and now. Shakespeare's plays reflect the passing intellectual and social fashions of his day as the plays of Bernard Shaw do of ours, and Shakespeare never minded in the least glancing at events or persons which were at the moment agitating the minds of his audience. No one can deny that he refers to the "war of the theatres" in the second act of *Hamlet*, or to the Irish campaign of Essex in one of the choruses of *Henry V*, or to the "dead shepherd" Marlowe in *As You Like It*, or to some entertainment given to Queen Elizabeth in the speech about the "little western flower" in *A Midsummer-Night's Dream*, or to the trial of the Jesuit, Henry Garnet, in the Porter's speech in *Macbeth*, or that the wreck of the "Sea Adventure" off an island in the Bermudas in 1609 gave him his idea for *The Tempest*—and so one could go on.

It is certain then that Shakespeare did not deliberately avoid topical allusion, as those who worship the Olympian claim. And if so, may we not suspect allusion and reference in many passages where it has hitherto not been detected? We not only may but should; for, once again, the essential Shakespeare will be altogether misconceived if we think of him as one who stood apart from the life of his time. On the contrary, we may look for him at the very heart of that life, and picture his eager spirit following the doings of Essex and Raleigh, of

Drake and Roger Williams, of Francis Bacon and Robert Cecil, with the keenest possible interest. Not "his tragic life-story", of which we know nothing, but the life at the courts of Elizabeth and James, the persons and doings of the great men of the land, the political and social events of the hour—these form the real background of his plays. But we must be careful not to be too crude or too literal in this matter, or we may fall into the trap that confounded Fleay. Shakespeare was a dramatic artist not a journalist, and above all he was subtle. He hardly ever goes out of his way to make a topical hit; he glances at the business in passing, obliquely and in hints, rather than by overt reference. And in so doing he showed a double wisdom: he escaped the troubles which fell upon dramatists who made open and direct attacks, since his "taxing like a wild-goose" might fly, "unclaimed of any man"; and, secondly, the passages in which the allusions occurred did not become dead wood which needed cutting out when the play was next revived and the events hinted at were forgotten; some of the meaning had evaporated, nothing worse. Of all the plays *Love's Labour's Lost* is that which abounds most in topicalities of this kind as it does also in indelicate innuendo, and those who obstinately hold to the doctrine of the impersonality and the respectability of Shakespeare should be condemned to edit that text until they had satisfactorily explained every allusion and every difficult reading.

But it is time I had done with criticising the portraits of Shakespeare by others and began my own.

It will, as is fitting, be a portrait in the renaissance style, though of an earlier period than that which stands at the beginning of this book. It will belong in manner to the Italian school which set its figures against a background of landscape and human occupation, of cloud-capped towers and solemn temples. And I shall begin by sketching this background first, not neglecting the central figure entirely, but showing it in outline only and leaving the details of posture, costume, face and expression to be filled in later. For though Shakespeare may be for all time, he was also very much of an age, and unless we grasp at least the main features of that age we are likely to miss much that is significant about him. Above all, his spiritual development, which is evident in the poems and plays, now we know their approximate order, can only be fully apprehended if we consider it in relation to the spiritual condition of the time in which he lived.

II

THE ELIZABETHAN SCENE

Infinite riches in a little room
Marlowe, *Jew of Malta.*

"THE SPACIOUS TIMES of great Elizabeth" has become a cliché since Tennyson first coined the phrase. Yet how "cabined, cribbed, confined", how "bound in to saucy doubts and fears" should we find ourselves in that world!

Shakespeare inhabited the diminutive, compact and tidy universe designed by Ptolemy fifteen hundred years before his day, and his very language is full of astronomical notions now long forgotten. This universe was a miracle of ordered harmony. A "pendent world", which included the whole starry space visible to man together with the containing Firmament, it hung like a jewel from the floor of Heaven, Hell lying beneath it and Chaos about it. Circular in shape, it comprised a system of transparent spheres, one within the other, in which were fixed the sun and moon, together with "those patens of bright gold" the stars, while the whole revolved at various speeds around "this centre" the earth, and in thus turning made music so ravishingly divine that mortals, closed in their "muddy vesture of decay", were unable to perceive it. We smile at this pretty little musical box, but it was more comforting to Man's pride and aspiration than our vast cosmos in which the earth is an infinitesimal atom. Of that old-time creation he was the masterpiece, "the beauty of the world, the paragon of animals"; and the grandeur and sublimity of Shakespeare's tragedies owe much to a sense of the kingly part Man was called upon to play "before high Heaven" on Earth, that central stage of a "wide and universal theatre".

Yet modern science, while reducing man to zero, has banished fear from his universe. In Shakespeare's limited cosmos fear met him at every turn. It only held together by keeping balance, harmony and an ordered hierarchy of degrees, corresponding with the angelic ranks about the Deity or the galaxy of nobles at an earthly court. Disturb this balance and at any moment the heavenly bodies might "start madly from their spheres"; and the dire effect of such "disasters" upon human affairs is described by Ulysses in the first act of *Troilus and Cressida*:

> Take but degree away, untune that string,
> And hark what discord follows! each thing meets
> In mere oppugnancy: the bounded waters
> Should lift their bosoms higher than the shores
> And make a sop of all this solid globe:
> Strength should be lord of imbecility
> And the rude son should strike the father dead.

The apprehension that the whole order might suddenly revert to Chaos haunted men's imagination; and is constantly in Shakespeare's thoughts.

> But I do love thee! and when I love thee not,
> Chaos is come again—

how much that cry of Othello's gains if we grasp what the Elizabethans meant by "the harmony of the spheres"! The stars, again, "rained influence", and astrologers spent busy lives searching the skies for evidence of their sway over the fortunes of individuals and of states, while unaccountable phenomena, like eclipses, comets and meteors, were especially dreaded,

> As harbingers preceding still the fates,
> And prologues to the omen coming on.

The world moreover was the abode of myriads of evil spirits, classified by learned demonologists and assigned to their respective elements of earth, air, fire and water. Madness was due to "possession", and there was a recognised procedure for the exorcising of devils by properly qualified persons. Dealers in black magic on the other hand, with their familiars and attendant demons, were held in detestation by all honest persons, and if convicted were burnt without mercy. Practically every one in Shakespeare's time believed in witchcraft, and we have no reason for thinking that the creator of *Macbeth* was immune from the universal delusions of his age. Among these must be reckoned ghost-lore, which was a topic of burning controversy in the sixteenth century, some believing that ghosts were devils and others adhering to the medieval idea that they were the spirits of the departed. Technically, all spirits, except angels and those in bliss, were evil. But popular superstition made an exception in the case of fairies, holding that they were "spirits of another sort". It is significant of this difference that while the fairies belong to Shakespeare's comedies, especially to those serenest of all his plays,

A Midsummer-Night's Dream and *The Tempest*, his tragic world is inhabited by ghosts and witches.

It is significant too that the ghosts and the witches do not become prominent until his Jacobean days, or at any rate until after 1600. The subjects of Elizabeth had a gaiety of mind that the next reign lacked. The Englishmen of her age felt that they did indeed belong to "spacious times". They had a sense of release, of new horizons suddenly opened up, which must have been extraordinarily exhilarating. The Renaissance was essentially an assertion of the spiritual emancipation of man from the religion, the social structure, the scholasticism of the middle ages. And in England during the second half of the sixteenth century special circumstances gave the movement a peculiar quality. The establishment of a strong central government, brought peace and order into a land which had groaned under the anarchy of the Wars of the Roses—and the fear of a return to such anarchy lies at the back of all Shakespeare's historical plays. The breach with Rome, although half the people still hankered after the forms and doctrines of the "old religion", typified the immense quickening of national self-consciousness that culminated in the triumphant defiance of the Spanish supremacy. A new nobility arose to take the place of the feudal baronage that finally perished on Bosworth field, a nobility based upon wealth, often derived from church property, or on royal favour, readily bestowed upon a handsome face and taking manners. The weakening of the bonds of custom which had tied the lower orders to status and the soil since time immemorial, caused the highways suddenly to grow populous with vagabond rogues and "lawless resolutes". The rapid development of internal trade and overseas commerce gave increased power and wealth into the hands of an expanding middle class. The drawing aside of the curtain of mystery veiling the stage of the Atlantic revealed to man's astounded and delighted gaze a whole New World for discovery, plantation, and plunder. And all these varied threads were woven together on Time's loom to fashion a texture of thought and society, which seemed at once durable and pliant, shot with swiftly changing hues and yet serviceable for daily wear, offering on the one hand security and on the other adventure. It was this combination—almost unparalleled in history since the days of Pericles—of social stability with illimitable opportunity for the individual, which gave the Elizabethan age its sense of balanced flight, its unique quality of happiness and spontaneity. The whole world was in flux, and yet by some trick of magic men trod on solid ground.

Nor were the Elizabethans in any doubt who the magician might be. They turned, and rightly turned, in gratitude to their Queen. Their grandfathers had endured the social anarchy which marked the end of the middle ages. Their fathers had drunk to the dregs the cup of Geneva under Edward VI and the cup of Rome under Mary, and found neither to their taste. Yet no third alternative had appeared possible. Elizabeth, the procrastinator, the crowned sphinx who could never make up her mind, who reigned forty-five years perpetually hesitating between Protestantism and Catholicism, between peace and war, between marriage and virginity, provided the alternative—a breathing-space of nearly half a century for the English people to discover a middle way and to grow contented, prosperous and respected throughout the world. England at that time was the one peaceful country in a Europe ravaged by religious wars, in which she was willing enough to take part on French or Flemish soil; and the epoch lies like a miraculous season of calm weather between the Wars of the Roses and the Puritan Revolution. The Virgin Queen was worshipped by her subjects because she gave them stability, and when foreign ambassadors enquired the secret of it she danced before them. The stability of Elizabethan England was a balance.

Her court too was both the keystone and the symbol of the national life. The headquarters of a strong executive under the permanent direction of the Cecils, it was also a stage on which almost any young man who took the Queen's fancy might cut a figure and if he were lucky make a fortune. Fortunes were to be had because the Crown not only controlled the distribution of lucrative monopolies and such properties as came to it through intestacy, but also itself took part in those expeditions, half-commercial and half-piratical, to the New World and elsewhere which were so frequent at this time. Elizabeth lived on the Thames; her five chief palaces, Whitehall, Hampton Court,

Greenwich, Richmond and Windsor, all gave on to the river; and she passed from one to another in her royal barge. The goings and comings, therefore, of the great sea-captains Frobisher, Hawkins, and Drake, took place under her very windows; and when the last-named returned to Deptford in 1580 after his famous voyage round the world, she boarded the *Golden Hind* and knighted him on his own deck, beneath which, as she pretended not to know, lay ballast in the form of ingots plundered from the Pacific coast of Spanish South America.

Nor was the traffic confined to America. Any day a vessel might appear in the Thames laden with merchandise from Africa, from Muscovy, from the Levant, even from India or the Far East. For London, which had been an obscure port at the north-west corner of the medieval map, suddenly found herself the centre of the world. And during the last fifteen years or so of Elizabeth's reign, eyes and ears greater than hers drank in the sights and sounds of the little-great river. Shakespeare's plays are drenched in sea-spray and shot with the coloured thread of mariner's tales, from the pitiful story of old Aegeon in *The Comedy of Errors* to *Pericles*, *The Winter's Tale* and *The Tempest*, while the Venice of his *Merchant* is only London in masquing attire.

The British Empire was founded by private adventurers exploiting the outlying parts of the world, with the unofficial encouragement of Elizabeth. Modern English literature had a similar origin. The Renaissance, though a learned movement, had its true centre not in universities but at courts grown rich with commerce. In the fourteenth and fifteenth centuries it became the fashion for the merchant princes of Italy to devote their surplus wealth, the banking system being then still in its infancy, to the encouragement of art and literature, much of which possessed the double attraction of offering at once a permanent investment and a means of personal display. This fashion spread to the rest of Europe, and Chaucer was already benefiting from it before 1400. Elizabeth, therefore, inherited a long tradition of royal patronage of art and letters, and as a daughter of Henry VIII and Anne Boleyn she was fond both of learning and of pageantry. But she inherited also an exhausted treasury and a full share of her grandfather Henry VII's passion for economy. Thus she contrived to obtain as much entertainment as possible without spending a penny more upon it than she could help.

The arrangement as regards plays was that towards Christmas, at which season and up to Twelfth Night the court held high festival, the Master of the Revels, whose office was a special department of the royal household under the immediate charge of the Lord Chamberlain, invited the acting-companies of London to submit plays for selection, very much as Philostrate does in *A Midsummer-Night's Dream*. The players, of course, received a fee for performing the chosen play or plays; but the Queen had no direct financial responsibility for their maintenance, any more than she had for the expeditions of Drake and Hawkins.

Indeed the public theatres of the metropolis came into existence during the second half of her reign in order, at any rate in theory, to give scope for the companies to rehearse before performing at court, without being at the charge of Her Majesty. And the theory that the players existed for the Queen's "solace", as the phrase went, was of vital importance in other respects. The growing puritanism of the City rendered the Lord Mayor and Corporation bitterly hostile as a rule to the theatre, so that but for the protection of the Court the stage would have been suppressed long before Shakespeare reached London.

The poets, like the dramatists, looked to Elizabeth as towards the sun in their heaven; but she had in general small comfort to offer those who courted her in verse and were unable to support themselves by public means. Moreover, she herself took much greater delight in music than in poetry, and had as we have seen a passion for dancing. In this, as in so many other ways, she was typically English of the time. During the latter part of her reign music and dancing were even more popular than the drama itself, and a puritan writer in 1587 complains that "London is so full of unprofitable pipers and fiddlers that a man can no sooner enter a tavern than two or three cast of them hang at his heels, to give him a dance before he depart". In those days you were entertained to music while your barber shaved you, and it was counted a shame for a lady or gentleman to be unable to "bear a part" when, as the custom was, the music-books were brought in after supper and the company sat round the table to sing madrigals. This indeed was the golden age of English music, and especially of English vocal music, the age of the great polyphonic composers William Byrd, Thomas Campian, Orlando Gibbons, and a host of others. That Shakespeare was himself passionately fond of music is witnessed by the countless references to music and singing in his plays.

Most of the well-known composers were in the service of noblemen, and every Elizabethan gentleman of standing maintained musicians as part of his household, "the music of the house" as Nerissa calls it being as necessary to greatness in that day as gardeners and chauffeurs are in this. The Tudor peace transformed the private armies of the barons, the bane of medieval England, into retinues of servants which included musicians, players and entertainers of other kinds; and instead of fighting each other the nobility, like Duke Theseus, occupied such time as was not given to the chase and other sports,

With pomp, with triumph and with revelling.

The great country houses, indeed, were in many ways like petty courts, and writers as well as musicians and players looked to their owners for patronage. Nor can there be any doubt that English literature, which might have fared badly had it been solely dependent upon Gloriana and her minister Burleigh, who preferred history and divinity to poetry and drama, stands very much indebted to the noble patrons of that period. Elizabethan authors, especially second-rate authors, frequently complain of lack of patronage; and with the multiplication of poets, novelists and pamphleteers, a number of them, no doubt, looked up and were not fed. But all the best poets and dramatists of the age seem to have found patrons, though the form of assistance they received may not have been always to their liking.

The career of Spenser is instructive. At first attached to the retinue of the Earl of Leicester, probably at the instance of his friend Sir Philip Sidney, who was Leicester's nephew, he next became private secretary to Lord Grey of Wilton, the Lord Deputy of Ireland, after which he held in succession various posts under the Irish government and so came to spend the rest of his life on "salvage soil", save for brief visits to London, one of them undertaken at the advice of yet another patron, Sir Walter Raleigh, who insisted on *The Faerie Queene* being presented at Court, where it earned the poet less than his hopes, but at any rate a pension of fifty pounds a year, a by no means inconsiderable sum for those days. Ben Jonson, to take another example, enjoyed the friendship, hospitality, and financial help of many patrons, and the Earl of Pembroke was in the habit of sending him £20 (equal to about £200 in modern money) every New Year for the purchase of books for his study.

In general, there seem to have been three degrees of patronage. First, there was the fee or reward for the dedication of a book, which varied in amount from shillings to guineas according to the generosity of the patron or the value he put upon the author's effort. Noblemen and gentry were pestered by impecunious authors for such fees, and refusals were no doubt common; but the custom was a time-honoured one and important publications seldom went without their rewards, sometimes from several patrons. The number of dedicatory sonnets to great personages which preface *The Faerie Queene* suggest, indeed, that Raleigh made it his business to collect as many guineas at Court for his friend as he could. And if the book pleased and its author were found acceptable, the next degree might be attained, namely personal employment in the patron's service. The hospitality which Spenser found at Leicester House, Ben Jonson for five years with Lord D'Aubigny, Nashe in the Isle of Wight with the family of Sir George Carey, and John Florio as servant of the young Earl of Southampton, was not of course entirely gratuitous. Literary men might prove useful in a variety of ways: they could act as secretaries, as land agents, as tutors to the patron or his children; and, when the occasion arose, they might be called upon to provide the "book" for a masque, a play, or some other form of entertainment, such occasions ranging from a wedding in the family to the elaborate preparations necessary for a visit from Her Majesty on one of her annual progresses. But the ultimate goal of most authors' ambition was the third and last degree of patronage, the gift of a permanent office under government. Very few attained it. Spenser, we have seen, did so, but only at the price of exile in a land he hated; Marlowe seems to have secured some shady employment in connexion with Walsingham's secret police system, and it cost him his life; Lyly hoped for the reversion of the mastership of the Revels Office, and died hoping.

Patronage, then, was not merely a custom of the age, it was for most writers an economic necessity. Every author sought for a patron, and the best patrons on their side thoroughly appreciated the compliment. For they stood to gain more than the services referred to above, which were after all merely incidental. What Shakespeare offered Southampton, and what all writers offered their patrons, was eternity.

> Not marble, nor the gilded monuments
> Of princes, shall outlive this powerful rhyme;
> But you shall shine more bright in these contents
> Than unswept stone besmeared with sluttish time—

such was the bid, and the terms in which Shakespeare expresses it remind us that patronage and the elaborate memorial monuments of the age belonged to the same fashion and were prompted by the same desire: to be remembered by succeeding generations. The investment was of course a speculation, since the length of the eternity depended upon the quality of the writer. Southampton is said to have ventured £1000, and if so posterity has paid him interest on the capital at an increasing rate of immortality; for fortune gave him the pick of the market.

Fashion and egotism, however, were not the whole story. The more distinguished Elizabethan and Jacobean courtiers were men of taste and culture who admired literature for its own sake and were as good judges of true poetic quality as their successors are of the points of a race-horse. And well they might be, for many of them were poets themselves in a minor fashion, and to be capable of journeyman's work is to be in the right way to appreciate the craft of a master. It generally flattered their vanity no doubt to feel that they had in their service poets as good or better than those of any of their rivals, and they made every effort to secure them. Yet there can have been little vanity in Sidney's love for Spenser, and when Raleigh brought Spenser to London in 1589 with three books of *The Faerie Queene* in his cloak-bag, he was inspired, partly by the hope of prestige for himself and favour from his royal mistress in return for this treasure-trove from Ireland, but partly also by real enthusiasm for what he recognised as genius of the highest order. Indeed Raleigh had an excellent eye for a poet, and appears to have lent his patronage to Marlowe, Chapman and Matthew Roydon simultaneously, to say nothing of mathematicians like Harriot for the study of navigation. And if Raleigh had poets and dramatists at command, the head of the rival faction at Court, the Earl of Essex, did no less. Thus the Montagues and Capulets of London had their attendant literary coteries, a fact which exerted an influence upon the career of Shakespeare so far all too little regarded.

While a dramatist, like Jonson, might enjoy the personal patronage of one nobleman, the actors he wrote for would in all probability be playing in the name of another. Every acting company served a lord, and was obliged to perform under his name and style, the lord being legally responsible for it. This was in the nature of a police measure, and differed in kind from personal patronage. Yet the two often shaded off into each other. The company's lord, for example, would naturally call upon them for help in providing entertainment at his own house; on the other hand, another lord might engage them for a similar purpose; occasionally, too, we hear of performances given in the public playhouse at the request of some gentleman or other.

Acting at the houses of private persons was generally in the evening, because public performances took place in the afternoon. It must not, however, be supposed that noblemen did not attend the public playhouses, though it was unseemly for ladies to show themselves there. A special "room", or as we should say "box", was reserved for lords, and we are told that during part of 1599, Shakespeare's patron, the Earl of Southampton, with his friend the Earl of Rutland, "passed away the time merrily in going to plays every day". Furthermore, the seats in the galleries, which were of varying prices, were largely occupied by gentlemen and professional men of different sorts, a large number of them being students of the Inns of Court, who, as one of them, the poet Donne, tells us, were

Of study and play made strange hermaphrodites.

Much has been heard of the "groundlings", for the

most part prentices, who paid a penny to stand on the floor of the house. It has been too little recognised that the public theatres were in the main dependent upon the cultured classes of London.

What would strike a modern eye most about Shakespeare's theatre was its smallness. The auditorium of the Globe was probably about 55 feet square, that is approximately the size of a lawn tennis court; and this included the stage, which jutted right out among the audience, and was some 43 feet wide by about 27 feet long. The play was therefore performed almost in the middle of the theatre, the groundlings standing on three sides of the stage, which was raised three or four feet off the floor, while the seats for those who could afford them were ranged in three tiers of galleries round the walls, and in some theatres stools could even be hired for accommodation on the stage itself. The whole atmosphere must have been extraordinarily intimate and domestic, especially when we remember that the personnel both of the company and of the audience was far more permanent than anything conceivable in modern London. Each member of the cast would be as familiar to the spectators as the individuals of a local football team are to-day to a crowd on the home ground. Under such conditions acting and drama were very different from anything we know now. And to understand Shakespeare, to follow the swiftness of his thought, the delicacy of his poetic workmanship, the cunning of his dramatic effects, the intricacy of his quibbles, to appraise in short the infinite riches of his art, we must think ourselves back into that little room at the Globe or its predecessors, in which his dramas were first given by a team of players, moving and speaking on a bare platform surrounded by a ring of faces only a few yards away, faces in front, to right, to left, above, faces tense with interest at the new miracle that awaited them, the faces of the brightest spirits and keenest intelligences of his time.

Did space permit, I might say much of the instrument for which he composed his mighty dramatic symphonies, that threefold instrument, the Elizabethan stage, the full significance of which Shakespearian criticism is only now beginning to appreciate. I will instance but one of its features, by way of showing how it moulded the art that belonged to it. The absence of stage scenery meant that Shakespeare had to create it in the verse he wrote.

> But look, the morn, in russet mantle clad,
> Walks o'er the dew of yon high eastward hill,

said an actor playing Horatio, pointing across the Globe theatre one sunny afternoon in 1601; and the spectators were entirely unconscious of any incongruity. Can we do better with all the resources of a mechanical age? Rather, does not the shining splendour of those lines make even the best contrivance of illuminated back-cloth look garish and absurd? Lacking scenery, again, Shakespeare lacked visual aids to the localisation of his scenes.

Where does *Macbeth* open, on earth or in hell? or the third act of *Julius Caesar*, before the senate house or within it? or the first and second scenes of the second act of *Romeo and Juliet*, inside the orchard of Capulet or beyond the wall? The answer to all these alternatives is that the action of Shakespeare's plays proceeds within the bare framework of the Elizabethan theatre, which just because it is delocalised allowed the dramatist a freedom denied to his modern successors. And if such bareness be thought a primitive crudity, let the military plays be considered, plays whose short fighting scenes followed each other on the Elizabethan platform with all the bustle and excitement of a battle-field seen simultaneously at many points, but are so sadly hampered by a drop-curtain as to be almost unplayable under our theatrical conventions. The supreme example of the kind is, of course, *Antony and Cleopatra*, in which the whole globe itself could be the scene because it was written for the Globe. In that theatre a dramatist was bounded in a nutshell and could count himself king of infinite space.

As with the theatre, so with the age. The "spaciousness" of Elizabeth's reign was in the minds of her subjects, not in their circumstances, most of which would seem small or mean to our thinking. No doubt the tiny city of London, with its spires nestling about old St Paul's, with its green fields to the north, and with the clear unembanked Thames lined with the palaces of the Queen and her great nobles, would seem very beautiful to us, could we survey it, through the smokeless air, from the trumpeter's hut surmounting the Globe on the southern Bankside, as Shakespeare himself had often done, and perhaps did in memory when writing Prospero's vision of towers and palaces and temples. But we should find much to offend nose and eye, to say nothing of humane feeling, in its narrow streets. With an aesthetic sensibility and discrimination that puts ours to shame, the Elizabethans combined a coarseness, brutality and physical insensitiveness, which it is essential to remember if we are to understand Shakespeare, whose growing abhorrence of these elements is the main key to his later development. And from the very beginning he brought from Stratford a delicate nose, which found the effluvia of London, human or otherwise, highly distasteful. Bodily ablutions and sanitation are inventions of nineteenth century England: a contemporary doctor advises his readers to confine their washing to the hands and wrists, to the face, the eyes, and the teeth, adding "in the night, let the windows of your house, specially of your chamber, be closed". Fresh air and sunlight were thought positively dangerous, ladies wearing masks to preserve their faces from the latter. Hygiene was in its infancy; the nostrums of medieval physic in their dotage. Surgery was a branch of the barber's art, and physiology was based upon the notion of humours which goes back to Hippocrates. In a word, man living in a pre-scientific age had no clue either to the prevention or to the cure of disease, with the result that the streets stank like middens, which indeed they were, and bubonic plague was an annual visitant to the city. The danger of infection was, however, well recognised, and when the deaths from plague reached more than fifty a week the theatres were closed by authority. A particularly violent outbreak in 1593–4, which killed some ten to fifteen thousand persons, had, as we shall see, an important influence upon Shakespeare's career, and other visitations affected the fortunes of his company.

The streets were turbulent as well as filthy and unhealthy. At any moment the cry of "Clubs!" would collect a mob of prentice boys for battle, and the Southwark scene in 2 *Henry VI* which begins

> *Alarm and Retreat. Enter again Jack Cade and all his rabblement.*
>
> *Cade.* Up Fish-street, down St Magnus' Corner, kill and knock down, throw them into Thames—

was assuredly from the life. Nor were poor prentices the only cause of strife. The brawls between the retainers of Montagues and Capulets had their parallel in London, for serving-men knew which way the wind blew and were ready enough to express in the streets the mutual hatred of their masters. Fighting and sport were near kindred. Close to the Globe stood the Bear Garden at which bears might be seen baited by dogs on most afternoons of the week except Sundays, while a scarcely more edifying display was provided by cock-fights; both royal sports which Elizabeth graced with her presence when they were given at court.

Even the crude justice of the age lent its aid to mob-excitement and brutalisation. The grisly decapitated heads of traitors looked down on you as you passed over London Bridge; this jeering procession that meets you is a throng following a cart, tied to the back of which walks a bawd, with beadles whipping her bare and bloody back; and if you are lucky you may find your way to Tyburn where a public execution is toward, of all spectacles the best-beloved by a London crowd. For here at no cost except a few hours of waiting to secure a good station, you may see the hangman at his work, of which hanging is the least interesting part. It is a common traitor, we will suppose, some Jesuit caught in his vestments at mass by Master Richard Topcliffe, the head of the government secret police, an expert human ferret, and cunning at devising new tortures. The Popish recusant has been dragged to Tyburn upon a hurdle, and the hangman, you hear, is in good form, having already shown marvels of skill with his knife upon other traitors before your arrival. For the Elizabethan hangman is an artist, and the knife is his chief instrument; the art consisting in tossing his man off the ladder, hanging him, but cutting him down before he breaks his neck, so that he may be dismembered and disembowelled while still alive. Indeed there is one recorded instance of a priest who was heard praying while the hangman already had his bleeding palpitating heart in his hand—and skill could hardly go beyond that. Did Shakespeare ever attend executions of this kind? Not often, I think; yet Macbeth's

3-2

cry, "As they had seen me with these hangman's hands!" shows that he could be present at least in imagination.

Less fascinating perhaps but more imposing was the pomp of executions for high treason, far the most important of which during Shakespeare's life in London being the beheading of Robert, Earl of Essex, on February 25, 1601, to which however the public were denied access, as it took place in the Tower. This portentous event, and not the death of the Queen in 1603, was the end of the true Elizabethan age, those halcyon days of happy ease, illimitable hope and untarnished honour, when Shakespeare was writing his great comedies and seemed able to turn a blind eye upon the squalor, the meanness, the bestiality around him. The brilliant but erratic young earl, the principal star in the Elizabethan firmament for the last ten years of the century, suddenly fell like Lucifer from heaven; and his catastrophe shook men's souls with terror and amazement as at some monstrous disaster in the skies. The sacred string of "degree" had been loosed; the harmony was broken; the Elizabethan balance overthrown. England awoke with a start to the grim realities of life, and the accession of James I ushered in a period of cynicism and gloom, self-indulgence and crime.

All this, we shall see, produced a profound effect upon Shakespeare. And how familiar it is to us! The modern world speaks a different language and has run a very different political course, but the mood of 1932 is almost exactly the mood of 1602;

for, though our material conditions are better, the height of our spiritual fall has been greater.

> Incertainty that once gave scope to dream
> Of laughing enterprise and glory untold,
> Is now a blackness that no stars redeem,
> A wall of darkness in a night of cold.

III

ENTER WILLIAM SHAKESPEARE
WITH DIVERS OF WORSHIP

What I have done is yours, what I have to do is yours, being part in all I have, devoted yours
Shakespeare to the Earl of Southampton, 1594.

SHAKESPEARE DIED at the early age of fifty-two, and history is almost completely silent concerning the first twenty-eight years of his life. Here is the meagre framework of certainties, drawn from ecclesiastical records:

1564, Ap. 26. William, son of John Shakespeare, baptised at Stratford.

1582, Nov. 27 and 28. Entries in the Bishop of Worcester's Register relating to the marriage of William Shakespeare to Anne Hathway of Stratford, a woman eight years his senior.

1583, May 26. Susanna, daughter to William Shakespeare, baptised at Stratford.

1585, Feb. 2. Hamnet and Judith, twin children to William Shakespeare, baptised at Stratford.

Thus we do not know how or where he was educated, when he joined the stage, at what period he went to London, or indeed anything at all of his boyhood or of those early critical years of adult life, beyond the fact of his marriage at eighteen to a woman of twenty-six. And then suddenly in the years 1592 to 1594 the curtain is drawn aside to discover him already at the height of fame and prosperity; as a leading actor in the leading company in England, as a member of the most brilliant of court

38

circles, as a poet whose publications were more sought after than those of any contemporary, and as a dramatist of such acknowledged power that one of the best-known dramatists of the day is found advising his fellow-playwrights to give up trying to compete with him. Surely there is no more dramatic entry in the whole of history than this of history's greatest dramatist.

Almost any conceivable interpretation may be placed upon the slender data of his career before 1592, and almost every conceivable interpretation has been. Fortunately we now know enough of the general life of Stratford and of the immediate circle in which he moved as a child to be able to rule out some of the extravagancies, and in particular the assumption, which as we saw underlies Sidney Lee's standard biography and which he derived from Halliwell-Phillipps, that Shakespeare was an ill-educated butcher-boy—"all but destitute of polished accomplishments" is Halliwell-Phillipps' phrase—whose education stopped at thirteen and who did not leave Stratford until he was twenty-three.

In the first place, Shakespeare was the son of well-to-do middle-class parents, and was therefore superior in station to Marlowe the son of a shoe-maker, Ben Jonson who was "brought up poorly" in a bricklayer's house, or Keats the son of a livery stableman, while he can claim at least equal rank with Spenser the son of a London clothier, Milton the son of a scrivener, and Wordsworth the son of a country attorney. His father, John Shakespeare, was in fact a prosperous wool-merchant, one of the leading citizens of Stratford-on-Avon, of which he was successively chamberlain or treasurer, alderman and in 1568, bailiff or mayor, in which year we find him making application to the College of Heralds for a coat of arms. His mother was the daughter of a wealthy farmer, himself probably connected with well-known gentlefolk of the county. It is necessary to emphasise these details, in order to combat the notion that Shakespeare grew up "with illiterate relatives and in a bookless neighbourhood", to quote Halliwell-Phillipps once again. There is plenty of evidence to show that other mercers of Stratford were well-educated and cultivated persons, and there is extant a letter in Latin written by a boy of eleven to his father who was a friend of the Shakespeares. Probably the most reliable picture of the life of these Stratford burgesses is that drawn by Shakespeare himself of the households of Master Page and Master Ford in *The Merry Wives of Windsor*, which as has well been said "might with equal propriety have been called *The Merry Wives of Stratford*".

John Shakespeare fell into trouble of some kind with the authorities about 1580, which led to his dropping out of the public life of the town for a while. This trouble was almost certainly due to his being a recusant, that is to say a member of the "old religion", who refused to attend church. And if so, it may have a bearing upon the schooling of William. We should naturally picture him attending the free grammar school of Stratford, where he

would have received a good education according to
the ideas of the age. On the other hand, there is
not a tittle of evidence to prove he went there, and
an ardent Catholic might well seek other means for
the education of his son than instruction at the
hands of a Protestant schoolmaster who was also a
clergyman. There were excellent alternatives to the
grammar school at that time, which would be fitter
nurseries for dramatic genius and more in keeping
with that passion for music which we know Shakespeare possessed. If, for example, he received his
education as a singing-boy in the service of some
great Catholic nobleman, it would help to explain
how he became an actor, since the transition from
singing-boy to stage-player was almost as inevitable
at that period as the breaking of the male voice in
adolescence. However this may be, it is certain
that the mature Shakespeare had somehow picked
up as good an education in life and the world's
concerns as any man before or since, and had acquired, if but "small Latin and less Greek", enough
to enable him to read and brood over his beloved
Ovid in the original. It is also, I think, clear that if
the author of *The Merry Wives of Windsor* knew his
middle classes, the author of *Love's Labour's Lost* had
made himself equally familiar with the life, manners
and conversation of ladies and gentlemen of the
land. To credit that amazing piece of virtuosity to
a butcher-boy who left school at thirteen, or even to
one whose education was nothing more than what
a grammar school and residence in a little provincial borough could provide, is to invite one either

to believe in miracles or to disbelieve in "the man of Stratford".

With most imaginative writers, memories of childhood and the natural scenes amid which they grew up are a primary source of later inspiration. It was so with Wordsworth; it was so with a very different writer, Dickens. It was certainly so also with Shakespeare. His poems and early plays are as full of Warwickshire sights and sounds and characters as Wordsworth's poems are full of the Lake country. The influence seems to ebb as he develops, and then returns in the last phase with redoubled force. And so, though we know nothing of his early life at Stratford, we can be certain of two things: first, that it made him a poet, and secondly, that it was the "fountain light" of his poetic vision.

We have no clue to Shakespeare's first appearance in London, and it is idle to spend time over legends of his holding horses' heads outside theatre doors or theories of employment in the offices of printers or lawyers. Nor do the dates of his marriage and the birth of his three children tell us anything about the time of his departure from Stratford. All they prove is that he must have been at home about August 1582, nine months before the birth of Susanna; in November of the same year for his marriage; and once again in the early summer of 1584, nine months before the birth of the twins. It may be a coincidence that the two vital dates here belong to the summer months; but it is at least worth remark that it was in the summer that plays were normally suspended in London because of the plague, so that

the dates referred to do not at all forbid us supposing
Shakespeare to have been already a professional
player at this period. Many have believed that he
made a regular practice throughout his career of
returning to Stratford for the summer season. In
any case—to nail one more slander to the counter—
there is no ground whatever for imagining that his
married life was an unhappy one, which is not the
same thing as saying that he himself was a model
husband; for, as Sir Edmund Chambers has put it,
"we cannot ascribe to Shakespeare that rigid propriety of sexual conduct, the absence of which in
more modern poets it has been too often the duty of
their family biographers to conceal". As to the "o'er-
hasty marriage" itself, followed by childbirth six
months later, that may be explained by the custom
of the time which recognised a solemn act of be-
trothal before witnesses as constituting marriage, a
so-called "pre-contract", the validity of which was
acknowledged by canon law and as a matter of fact
is insisted upon by Shakespeare himself, since the
plot of *Measure for Measure* turns on Angelo's
tyranny in condemning Claudio for marrying
Juliet in just this fashion.

We cannot tell what happened, then, in the first
act of his career as a dramatist. But it is legitimate to
suppose that there was a first act, since, when we find
a man of thirty already near the top of his particular
tree, we must assume some previous climbing.
Romances have been written about "Shakespeare's
lost years in London"; it is more profitable to turn to
the second act which dates from the year 1592.

At its opening we find ourselves by the squalid death-bed of Robert Greene, playwright and profligate, the most productive of those university wits who about 1585 captured the London stage and founded the popular Elizabethan drama. In a literary testament to "his fellow-scholars about this city", which he entitled *A Groatsworth of Wit, bought with a million of repentance*, and which was published early in September, 1592, he appealed to Marlowe, Peele and a "young Juvenal", who is usually identified with Nashe, to surrender the vain art of play-making and trust no longer to the players,

For there is an upstart Crow, beautified with our feathers, that with his *Tiger's heart wrapt in a Player's hide*, supposes he is as well able to bumbast out a blank verse as the best of you; and being an absolute *Johannes factotum*, is in his own conceit the only Shake-scene in a country. O that I might entreat your rare wits to be employed in more profitable courses, and let those Apes imitate your past excellence, and never more acquaint them with your admired inventions.

The pun in "Shake-scene" leaves no doubt that Shakespeare is meant; the parody of "O tiger's heart wrapt in a woman's hide", a line from the fourth scene of the first act of 3 *Henry VI*, shows that Greene associated that play with him; the phrase "upstart Crow beautified with our feathers" has been taken by most (until quite recently) as a charge of plagiarism; while the rest of the attack is an unwilling tribute at once to Shakespeare's success and his versatility. Even more interesting is a later comment upon it by Henry Chettle, at this time

44

a printer, who, having himself edited Greene's pamphlet, felt bound, in a book of his own published at the beginning of December, to offer a handsome public apology. After confessing that he knew nothing of Shakespeare personally when he passed Greene's book for press, he continues:

> I am as sorry as if the original fault had been my fault, because myself have seen his demeanour no less civil than he excellent in the quality he professes. Besides, divers of worship have reported his uprightness of dealing, which argues his honesty, and his facetious grace in writing that approves his art.

These two references have been quoted and discussed hundreds of times; and no wonder, for they are the only personal allusions to Shakespeare we possess before 1598 and far the most significant that have come down to us from his contemporaries, except perhaps the remarks of Ben Jonson. Nevertheless it is doubtful whether their full meaning has even yet been grasped.

Chettle's emphasis upon Shakespeare's "uprightness of dealing" and "honesty" are pointless unless they are connected with Greene's phrase "beautified with our feathers". There have been attempts of late to show that Greene was merely angry with Shakespeare as a player who dared to compete as a dramatist with "scholars about this city" and that he had no intention of accusing him of stealing their plays. Such attempts have ignored Chettle's apology as they have also tended to belittle lines by one R.B. printed in 1594, which prove that one contemporary at any rate had no doubt of Greene's meaning. For my part, R.B.'s words

> Greene gave the ground to all that wrote upon him.
> Nay more, the men that so eclipsed his fame
> Purloined his plumes, can they deny the same?—

make it certain that there is substance of some kind in the traditional notion of Shakespeare as, at least in his early days, the reviser of other men's dramas.

Nor is there anything dishonourable about this. Once the "book" of a play had been purchased from a dramatist by an acting company, it became their absolute property, and if they afterwards had the play improved or refurbished, no one had any reason to object either in law or equity. It was a thing constantly done, and the London theatre-manager Henslowe freely employed one dramatist to "mend", "alter" or make "additions" to an old "book" written by another. What was new about Shakespeare, and alarming to dramatists dependent for their living upon commissions from the players, was that he was himself an actor, would be prepared to write new plays and revise old ones for his own company, and thus seemed to be taking the bread out of their mouths. Greene prefaces his outburst by declaring that he had been "forsaken" by the players, and it was natural for him, dying penniless and in abject misery, to attribute his condition in part to this player-dramatist who had not only robbed him, as he thought, of his occupation, but was rendering obsolete his plays by re-writing them, only too successfully. Whether he also intended to imply that Shakespeare was "writing upon" Marlowe, Peele, and Nashe as well, and that 3 *Henry VI* was one of the plays involved, must be left here an open question. What he says makes certain, I think, that by 1592 Shakespeare is actively engaged in writing plays, which are proving a great success; that these plays are of many kinds (for so I interpret "Johannes factotum"); that some at least of them are based upon the work of other men; and that theatrically speaking he is a portent, inasmuch as he is not a university man or professional dramatist but an ordinary player, working as a sharer or hireling for a company. Greene's word "upstart" and Chettle's remark that he knew nothing of Shakespeare previously, have inclined some to believe that he had only recently joined the stage or come to London. The deduction is unwarranted; Chettle also professes ignorance of Marlowe, who had been a successful playwright for years, while "upstart" refers, I think, rather to Shakespeare's status than to his advent.

It is common sense to suppose that Shakespeare had won his spurs as a player and a dramatist before being allowed to re-shape work by so famous a writer as Greene, and this implies a period of apprenticeship previous to 1592. In what company or companies he served is unknown, but most authorities believe that in 1592 he was working for Lord Strange's Men who had lately beaten the Queen's Men out of the field both at court and in popular favour. Now Greene was the chief writer for the Queen's Men and if the "upstart crow" was responsible for their defeat by Strange's Men,

that would be a further cause for bitterness. Moreover, the plague raged during the years 1592–4 so
severely that the theatres were closed for most of
the period, with disastrous results to many companies, some of whom were forced to sell those most
precious of their possessions, the MS. playbooks
from which they acted. It is probable that many
playbooks of the kind passed into the hands of
Shakespeare and his fellow actors during these years.
It must be remembered too that by a strange fate the
principal dramatists who had hitherto entertained
London—Lyly, Greene, Kyd, Peele, Lodge, Marlowe—all either died or left the stage, for one cause or
another, about this time. Thus luck as well as genius
contributed to Shakespeare's success; the critical
years 1592–4, so unkind to his rivals, were his
opportunity both as a dramatist and also, we shall
see, as a poet.

But let us return to Chettle's apology. We may
learn from it that Shakespeare in 1592 was a very
charming person. Chettle had obviously met him
some time between September and December,
and pays a tribute to his bearing which reminds us
strongly of the testimony to him as "honest and of
an open and free nature" which Jonson left among
his papers forty-five years later. Shakespeare had
just ground for complaint, but he bears no malice,
and politely accepts Chettle's explanation and
apology. Chettle moreover backs his own tribute
with a reference to the high esteem in which Shakespeare is held by "divers of worship" who admire
both his character and "his facetious grace in

writing". This brings me to my most important point about these two references. For, that "divers of worship" or, as we might now say, several persons of rank and position, should intervene in this quarrel between a dead dramatic lion and an upstart crow, argues that the crow possessed powerful friends who thought him worth their support; in other words that already in 1592 Shakespeare had his admirers in high places. As for the "facetious grace", could better words be found to describe those qualities in Shakespeare's early comedies which would especially appeal to the cultured men of rank that Chettle seems to refer to?

I shall presently make suggestions about these worshipful gentlemen. But apart from personal identification, it is certain I think that Shakespeare wrote with his eye particularly upon men of such a kind; for, as he tells us in *Hamlet*, in his opinion their "censure", that is to say their judgment, must "o'er-weigh a whole theatre of others". It is easy also to guess from the fare he provided that these noble patrons were young. Play after play at this period contains its party of dashing young bucks. They come abroad to see the great world in *The Two Gentlemen of Verona*, *The Comedy of Errors* and *The Taming of the Shrew*. They seek to combine this with university studies in the last named, or they found a little "academe" of their own in *Love's Labour's Lost*. Or yet again, as in *The Merchant of Venice* and *Romeo and Juliet*, they are just men about the town or gentlemen about the court, revelling and roistering and chaffing each other.

Almost always too, like young men of whatever rank or period, they hunt in threes. Mercutio, Romeo, and Benvolio: Berowne, Longaville, and Dumain; Antonio, Bassanio, and Gratiano; Petruchio, Lucentio, and Tranio—so persistent is the triangle that it is hard to resist a suspicion that the same triangle existed among the "divers of worship" for whose eyes and ears they were primarily intended.

And how large a proportion of the dialogue in early Shakespearian comedy is taken up with young-mannish conversation! These students, courtiers, or inns-of-court men—always thoroughly English and of London, whatever be the name of the Italian city to which they ostensibly belong—chat together, or with their servants, worrying the language and getting entangled in it, like puppies with a ball of string. They quibble and jest, endlessly and untiringly, while their jesting, after the manner of undergraduates, is frank and unseemly. They skirt philosophy, write poems and read them aloud, and above all discuss love, discuss it lightly, sometimes cynically, often indecorously. For the atmosphere is essentially a bachelor one, and the general attitude towards the great enemy of that state is best expressed in the words of the serving-man in *The Two Gentlemen of Verona*: "Though the chameleon Love can feed on air, I am one that is nourished by my victuals and would fain have meat".

As a precipitate for this atmosphere, and as whetstones for these blades, Shakespeare introduces his "mocking wenches"—a type which he invented, and reproduced with variations in one play after

50

another. And there can be no doubt that his "facetious grace" appeared most brilliant to his contemporaries in the "sets of wit well played" between the young bachelors and these sprightly women-folk. *Love's Labour's Lost* is richest in this dialogue, is indeed little more than a succession of such "sets of wit"; but it is to be found, of course, in many other plays. Petruchio and Katherine, for instance, carry on an elaborate duel of the kind at their first encounter. Skirmishes of this sort are more exciting than mere "volleys of words" shot off by the men among themselves, since the element of sex gives a sense of danger to the fencing; the buttons are off the foils, a slip and one or other may be wounded—to the heart. It pleased Shakespeare to underline this peril, so to speak, by steeping his dialogue in *double entendre*. The conversation is not coarse, as it often is between the men, but it is frequently highly indelicate, though the equivocal sense is generally so obscure as to escape the casual modern reader entirely, and must sometimes also have escaped all but the keenest witted amongst the judicious in the original audience.

Nor was it with wit alone that he entertained them. This Johannes factotum was prepared to try everything, and in everything carried it off, as if indeed he were "the only Shake-scene in a country". What comedies could be more different from *Love's Labour's Lost* or from each other than *A Midsummer Night's Dream*, *Two Gentlemen of Verona*, *The Comedy of Errors*, and *The Taming of the Shrew*? the first as dainty a piece of dew-starred cobweb as ever caught the moonshine's watery beams, the second a courtly romance of love and friendship, the third a knock-about Plautine farce—an admirable piece of stage-craft, and the fourth a lively study of Italian bourgeois manners cunningly let into a framework of English provincial life with its drunken tinker and its merry lord. And there were varieties of tragedy also: *Titus Andronicus* (if this be Shakespeare's), a generous banquet of blood in a style as fashionable with the intellectuals of that day as tales of crime and detection are with those of ours; *Richard III* ministering to the same taste with its magnificent Machiavellian villain; and lastly *Romeo and Juliet*, one of the three or four supreme love-poems of the world, which at once became Shakespeare's favourite play with young Englishmen and remained so at any rate down to the outbreak of the Civil War, if we can judge from the condition of its text in the Bodleian copy of the First Folio at Oxford, which was almost thumbed to pieces by eager students of the seventeenth century.

This tragic tale of star-crossed lovers reveals much both of the young Shakespeare and of the audience he set out to please. Written at the height of his Elizabethan gaiety, it is shot with comic colour; indeed the first two acts are almost pure comedy, Mercutio and the Nurse standing out pre-eminent. By what right, it may be asked, have these reprobates thrust themselves into so tender, so sublime a drama of young love? The answer is that they are the two main pillars which support the whole dramatic structure. For the lovers, in the great scenes where they are together, chant their passion to each other but tell us little about themselves. Shakespeare had to assure us that they are creatures of common clay, a real boy and girl, not just mouthpieces of the passion he gives them. He accomplishes this by placing characters of almost outrageous vitality by their sides—the Nurse with Juliet and Mercutio with Romeo. It is their function also to remind us time and again of the physical basis of love; for he is full of bawdy talk such as hot-blooded young men affect, while she prattles as old peasant women will. Do such passages grate? are they just "sallets to make the matter savoury" for a debased and barbarous audience? It was not the "groundlings" alone among Shakespeare's spectators who laughed at them, and modern readers who regard them as wanton excrescences upon an otherwise perfect love-poem are missing the point. The magician is assuring us, once again, of reality. He is proving that the marvellous blossom of love which forms the main theme of the story is not a mere poet's dream, a pleasing fancy, but a piece of real life rooted deep in the crude common soil of humanity, the soil we all know so well, too well. He is persuading the young of his audience that the passion of Mercutio's bosom friend for a mistress suckled at the Nurse's breast is a passion possible for themselves.

It is just because Shakespeare conceals nothing and condemns nothing—because he is so utterly unlike a schoolmaster or a preacher—that the young then and the young now feel safe with him. And having gained their confidence, he may lead them where he will, to endure the purging fires of *Macbeth* and *Othello*, to share the crucifixion and redemption of Lear, to win through to the haven of atonement and forgiveness in the enchanted island.

And if *Romeo and Juliet* and *Love's Labour's Lost*, together with the other early plays, belong especially to the young, still more is this true of the poems and the sonnets which are closely connected with them both in time and mood, as the large number of parallels in word and image prove. In 1592, Shakespeare was beating his rivals and winning to his allegiance "divers of worship" in London by his "facetious grace" as a playwright. But it was as a poet he first really took the town by storm, with the publication, in April 1593, of *Venus and Adonis*, seven editions of which appeared in the decade 1593–1602. There is plenty of evidence that he was best known by this, and its successor *The Rape of Lucrece*, among the reading public right down to the end of Elizabeth's reign, which is not perhaps surprising when we remember that these two poems were the only Shakespearian productions available in print until 1597, at which date the series of quarto texts of the plays began with the pirated *Romeo and Juliet* to be followed shortly by *Richard III*, *Richard II*, *Love's Labour's Lost*, and 1 *Henry IV*.

The publication of *Venus and Adonis* must have produced an effect upon London in 1593 not unlike that which the First Series of Swinburne's *Poems and Ballads* created in 1866, except that Shakespeare put himself at the head of a fashion instead of initiating one. When *Poems and Ballads* "fell like a thunderbolt upon Philistia", the youth of England were tired of the "lilies and langours" of Tennyson, and turned with delight to the "roses and raptures" the new poet offered. In the same way, to understand the popularity of *Venus and Adonis*, we must remember that, since the appearance in 1579 of *The Shepheard's Calender*, the puritan Spenser had been the dominant star in the poetic heavens, and that in 1590 he began the publication of *The Faerie Queene*, the ostensible purpose of which, with its Book I on "Holiness", its Book II on "Temperance", and its Book III on "Chastity", was to "fashion a gentleman or noble person in virtuous and gentle discipline". Shakespeare's retort to Spenser's destruction of the Bower of Bliss was *Venus and Adonis*, in which "sweet desire" was given divine honours, and her rites exhibited according to the example of Ovid, a quotation from whom stands on the title-page of the book. The poem is the supreme example of what may be called the Elizabethan "fleshly school of poetry". Yet there is nothing whatever Swinburnian about it. The note of revolt, of craving for forbidden fruit, is entirely absent: the "roses and raptures" are not of vice, but of a frank acceptance of what Rossetti called "the passionate and just delights of the body". It is at times laboured and at others a little stuffy, but in its defects as in its merits, in its pictorial quality and in its loading of every rift with ore, it reminds us more of the young Keats, the Keats of *Endymion*, than of any other poet.

As with Keats too, the passion for Beauty, less

explicit than the fleshly passion, is so all-pervading
as to remain our abiding impression when the book
is closed and the details fade from the memory. It
comes out most in those references to country life
and animals in which the poem abounds. These
glimpses of Stratford are indeed so much happier
than the descriptions of the efforts by amorous Venus
to awaken passion in her Adonis, that it is not
difficult to see where Shakespeare's heart lay. Yet
even in the wanton passages his feet often move to
such bewitching measures that one is ravished by
the witchery into forgetting the wantonness. The
same happy passion pulses through the *Sonnets*, and
Beauty is sometimes so closely identified in the
poet's mind with the patron he celebrates that they
become one.

> From fairest creatures we desire increase
> That thereby beauty's Rose might never die

are the opening lines, and they announce the theme
of the series. But perhaps a play, a play where
some would least expect it, contains the best of all
Shakespeare's hymns to Beauty. *Love's Labour's
Lost* is full of talk of ladies and their bright eyes; and
it is given to Berowne, the arch-heretic, to reveal
their mystic significance in his great speech of
recantation.

> But Love, first learnéd in a lady's eyes,
> Lives not alone immuréd in the brain,
> But with the motion of all elements,
> Courses as swift as thought in every power,
> And gives to every power a double power,
> Above their functions and their offices.
> It adds a precious seeing to the eye—

56

A lover's eyes will gaze an eagle blind;
A lover's ear will hear the lowest sound
When the suspicious head of thrift is stopped;
Love's feeling is more soft and sensible
Than are the tender horns of cockled snails;
Love's tongue proves dainty Bacchus gross in taste.
For valour, is not Love a Hercules,
Still climbing trees in the Hesperides?
Subtle as Sphinx, as sweet and musical
As bright Apollo's lute, strung with his hair;
And when Love speaks, the voice of all the gods
Make heaven drowsy with the harmony.
Never durst poet touch a pen to write,
Unless his ink were tempered with Love's sighs.

Love for Shakespeare, in short, is a symbol of that passionate apprehension of Beauty, which sets all five senses afire and is the great gift of the poet and the artist to his fellows. And at this time he was so drunk with Beauty that he saw her everywhere, and was ready to worship her epiphany in anything or anybody he met.

Here, I believe, is the real explanation of his attitude towards his patron. The passion of poets, "endued with more lively sensibility, more enthusiasm and tenderness" than ordinary men, must be accepted for truth, however strange it may seem. The world with much difficulty has learned to credit Wordsworth's

To me the meanest flower that blows can give
Thoughts that do often lie too deep for tears.

Why does it suspect flattery when Shakespeare writes of a young and cultivated nobleman, known to have been one of the handsomest and most fascinating figures at the court of Elizabeth,

Shall I compare thee to a summer's day?
Thou art more lovely and more temperate.

Accept the *Sonnets*, and we must believe that the nineteen-year-old Earl of Southampton, to whom as is now generally believed they were addressed, was the most splendid and captivating human being that Shakespeare had yet seen, and that he paid him the devotion of a whole heart. In that age of fulsome adulation, Shakespeare is a marvel of restraint and self-respect. Almost every play he wrote gave him opportunities of flattering the reigning monarch, and it would have been very much to his interest and to that of his company had he done so. Yet the only reference to Elizabeth is the lovely but almost frigid passage about the "imperial vot'ress" in *A Midsummer-Night's Dream*, so cool indeed that I have sometimes wondered whether there is not just a touch of malice in it. As for James I, Shakespeare pays court to his interests in *Macbeth*, but nowhere does he offer that incense of blandishment which the royal nostrils delighted in. In the *Sonnets* he does not flatter; he writes in love and admiration.

Admiration; yes, and reverence; for however much the youth might admit him to his gracious intimacy, a whole social hierarchy divided the player from the earl. Helena, the physician's daughter, says of Bertram, the young count:

'Twere all one
That I should love a bright particular star
And think to wed it, he is so above me:
In his bright radiance and collateral light
Must I be comforted, not in his sphere—

58

a passage which exactly defines the social relationship between Shakespeare and his patron. In our
day it is impossible for us to enter into the emotional
implications of all this—and with poetry it is just
those implications that matter most—though what
millions of people in this country feel for the Prince
of Wales may furnish a clue. And yet, if we do not,
we may fail to understand not only the *Sonnets* in
general but those curious sections of them which
concern "the Dark Lady".

The subject is far too obscure and difficult to
embark upon here; but, as everyone knows, one
point emerges beyond dispute, namely that the
poet introduces the patron to his mistress and
that the two then play him false. Shakespeare
expresses his grief, and there even seems to
be a cooling of affection for a time. Nevertheless,
the sonnet-letters continue, and presently become
as glowing as before. It may well be that his
affection for Southampton was more to him than his
passion for the mistress, who as appears from the
sonnets written to her held him by little more than
physical attraction. But I think too that, deeply as
he could enter into the soul of jealousy in his tragic
period, it probably never occurred to him to be
jealous of his "bright particular star". The sonnet
beginning

Take all my loves, my love, yea take them all

has an abject, almost a cringing, sound to modern
ears; yet the friendship that is ready to sacrifice love
itself on the altar of its ideal is a common-place of

59

the Renaissance, to which Shakespeare has given dramatic expression in that strange last scene of *The Two Gentlemen* where Valentine is prepared to offer Silvia to Proteus the moment after he has rescued her from being violated by him. And while the "two gentlemen" of Verona are equals in rank, Shakespeare was a player and Southampton an earl. In any case, to suppose that the player was acting merely from motives of self-interest, because he undoubtedly gained much even financially from his "service" to the earl, is to contradict everything we know of his character and conduct in other relations.

But I am in the middle of a story, the beginning of which has not yet been told. Thanks largely to the writings of Mr J. A. Fort, what used to be called the "mystery of the *Sonnets*" has now in the main, I think, been solved. He noticed, as all have, that while *Venus and Adonis*, which belongs to April 1593, was dedicated to Southampton in respectful terms, the tone of the dedication of *The Rape of Lucrece*, published in May 1594, was so much warmer that we may legitimately assume a considerable increase of intimacy between the two men during the interval. He noticed further that sonnet 104 makes clear that Shakespeare had first met his patron, in the spring, three years before this particular sonnet was written; and, assuming very plausibly that the first meeting of poet and patron was on the occasion of the presentation of *Venus and Adonis*, he arrived at the conclusion that Shakespeare began writing sonnets to Southampton immediately after the latter's acceptance of his poem, that the friendship

thus begun ripened rapidly, and that the first
hundred and four sonnets give a poetic account of
it from the spring of 1593 to the spring of 1596. His
theory has since received support from Dr G. B.
Harrison who has shown grounds for believing that
sonnet 107, with its line "The mortal moon hath
her eclipse endured" is a reference to the universal
fears for Queen Elizabeth's health in 1596, fears
that proved illusory when on September 7th she
completed her sixty-third or "climacteric" year,
which all the best astrological opinion held to be
peculiarly dangerous. Thus the bulk of the *Sonnets*,
including those concerned with the incident of the
"Dark Lady", must have been written between
April 1593 and September 1596.

But if Shakespeare did not meet Southampton
until April 1593, who were the worshipful gentlemen Chettle is alluding to in December 1592? To
answer this question properly would involve a
lengthy argument concerning one of the most de-
batable periods of Shakespeare's life, which is quite
beyond the scope of this book. I propose, therefore,
to conclude the present chapter by stating briefly the
views I have so far arrived at about Shakespeare's
doings in the years 1592 to 1594, and if the reader
will please remember that they are largely con-
jectural and likely to be stoutly contested by others,
he should take no harm.

When Greene attacked the "upstart crow" from
his death-bed, the said upstart was, as I have
already suggested, an actor-playwright working for
Lord Strange's Men. Ferdinando Stanley, Lord

Strange, was a remarkable personage, a patron much courted by poets, a man of strong Catholic leanings, and a friend of the Queen's brilliant favourite, the Earl of Essex. This friendship, I believe, helps to account for the sudden rise of Lord Strange's players during 1591–3 into court favour. In any case, both Strange and Essex would be quick to appreciate the "facetious grace" of the young dramatist. And if Greene's scurrilous pamphlet reached their hands, what more likely than that one of them should dispatch an emissary to the publisher, Chettle, telling him that this kind of thing was going too far and must stop? Possibly the emissary was no other than Shakespeare himself, bearing a sharply worded letter from his patron, and smoothing matters over for Chettle by his own charming manners.

But Shakespeare and his fellow-players were presently in need of still greater assistance than protection from posthumous malice. The years 1592–4, as I have said, are the worst recorded plague-years of Elizabeth's reign, and the public theatres were closed by authority during the whole twenty-four months after June 1592, except for two brief seasons. This spelt disaster for the acting profession, which could only maintain itself by public performance, and though some companies eked out a kind of living by touring the provinces, others went under or were forced to amalgamate with former rivals. In these straits, Shakespeare's mind naturally turned towards the possibilities of literary patronage, described in Chapter II. His friends at court lent him their advice; overtures were made to the *fidus Achates* of Essex, the attractive and immensely wealthy young Earl of Southampton; *Venus and Adonis* was written during the winter of 1592–3, and presented in person the following April; the meeting delighted both parties—and Shakespeare had secured not merely a patron but a revered and beloved friend. That before he met him he was in touch with persons who had Southampton's interests at heart is, I think, proved by the fact that both *Venus and Adonis* and the first seventeen sonnets, which I conjecture were presented with that poem, are advice to the young earl to marry; a step which to the chagrin of his friends and relations, who wanted an heir, he was at the time refusing to take. The advice is obvious enough in the *Sonnets*, but in allegorical fashion it is present in the longer poem also, if we take Adonis, who rejects the advances of Venus and perishes by an early death, as a warning. Indeed, the lines

> For he being dead, with him is beauty slain,
> And, beauty being dead, black chaos comes again

are an epitome of the opening series of the *Sonnets*.

It is significant that Shakespeare should first have approached his patron in the capacity of adviser, since that is the part, I believe, he played throughout with his friends at court. He offered them counsel; offered it as only a dramatist could, by holding the mirror up to nature and showing them, if they had eyes to see, "virtue her own feature, scorn her own image, and the very age and body of the time his form and pressure"; offered it respectfully, unobtrusively, but candidly and with admirable discretion, though if matters grew desperate and they proved blind and deaf, he was capable of blunt plain-speaking.

Southampton accepted the counsellor, who was ten years his senior, whatever he may have thought of the counsel. The marked change of tone in sonnet 18 and in the dedication to *The Rape of Lucrece* point to an intimacy which can, I think, only be explained by close association. In other words, I suggest that soon after the first meeting Shakespeare passed on to what I have called in Chapter II the second degree of patronage, that is to say he accepted personal service as a member of the earl's household and remained with him for most of 1593 and part of 1594. There is a well-authenticated tradition that Shakespeare was at one time a "schoolmaster in the country". This tradition may refer to his stay at Titchfield, Southampton's seat, during this period, in the capacity of a tutor. We know that the earl had one tutor in residence with him, John Florio, the translator of Montaigne, whose influence upon Shakespeare has been remarked by many critics; and if the dramatist acted as Florio's colleague for some months, his interest in the great French humanist would be explained. If also Baptista in *The Shrew* could entertain two "schoolmasters", one in languages and poetry, the other in music and mathematics for his daughters, we need not be surprised to find two tutors for the instruction of a wealthy young nobleman. Many, again, have supposed that Shakespeare paid a visit to Italy during this period—the intimate knowledge he shows in the plays of the topography of Venice certainly suggests more than hearsay. What better way of his going there can be thought of than in company with the young earl and Giovanni Florio?

Shakespeare's main occupation at Titchfield, I suggest, was to provide entertainment, and especially dramatic entertainment, for which Southampton had a passion. He could do this the more easily that his fellow-players, kicking their heels in London because of the plague, would be ready to assist him if he lifted a finger. And there is one play by Shakespeare, obviously intended for private performance, which I think was undoubtedly written during this period for the delight of Southampton, and probably of Strange, Essex, and others of the circle as well. The play is *Love's Labour's Lost*.

Allusions and borrowings indicate that it was composed for a performance at Christmas 1593, and it must have been given at a private house since there was no play at court that Christmas, and all the theatres were closed. Moreover, the play, as is now generally recognised, is from beginning to end a burlesque upon the adherents of Sir Walter Raleigh, who is himself probably caricatured in the figure of the fantastical Spaniard, Armado. The Essex party in 1593 were triumphant over their rival; for in May 1592 it was discovered that Raleigh had committed an offence with one of the Queen's maids-of-honour which in the eyes of Elizabeth was almost equivalent to high treason. He was banished from court, and did not again

kiss hands until June 1597. An extravaganza,
with Raleigh and his minions as comic characters,
would be perfectly safe. Shakespeare was not, however, afraid to introduce other persons also; for it
is my belief that in Ferdinand, King of Navarre,
Berowne, Longaville, and the "young Dumain",
the spectators were intended to see stage-reflexions
—not of course portraits—of Ferdinando Stanley,
who had become Earl of Derby and King of Man
in September 1593, the Earl of Essex, who had been
fighting side by side with Biron, or as the English
called him, Berowne, on French soil in 1591,
Southampton himself, and the young Earl of Rutland who was at this date seventeen years old.
Essex, Southampton, and Rutland formed a trio of
close friends, and it is this trio, I think, that Shakespeare has chiefly in mind in those bachelor plays
I have referred to above. Stanley, an older man,
died in April 1594, and so drops out.

A year after *Love's Labour's Lost* was played,
Shakespeare has returned to the public stage; the
plague is over; and he is found as one of the leading
men of a new company, the Lord Chamberlain's
men, acting before the Queen at court. I associate
these events with Southampton's coming of age on
October 6, 1594, when his property would for the
first time be his own. Then, if ever, he made that
munificent gift of money to Shakespeare which
tradition, probably exaggerating, puts as high as
£1000. We are told that the gift was "to enable him
to go through with a purchase which he heard he
had a mind to". Even had the sum been only £100,

it would have made it possible for Shakespeare to get together this new company and set it on its legs. The company was already formed in June and was touring in September; but on October 8, two days after Southampton came of age, we find it in occupation of a London theatre. In a word, I suggest that the patronage of Southampton proved not only a refuge for Shakespeare and some of his fellow-actors in the disastrous years of the plague, but the foundation of their fortunes in the period that followed.

Of the later relations between the dramatist and his patron it is difficult to speak with any kind of assurance. The *Sonnets* continue until 1596, and if after that there are few of them this may be explained by Shakespeare's herculean labours for his company and by Southampton's advance in years. The earl, however, retained to the full his passion for the theatre, and I have already quoted evidence of this from the year 1599. How the rebellion and fall of Essex affected matters can only be guessed, but it is at least significant to find Southampton and Burbadge associated together in 1604 for the production of that anti-Raleigh play, *Love's Labour's Lost*, before the consort of James I, Queen Anne. It is even possible that Shakespeare's interest in the sea, which is so evident in his last plays, and his references to colonisation in *The Tempest*, may be connected with Southampton's own interest in Virginia at this period.

IV

CHARACTER AND COMEDY

> His voice was propertied
> As all the tunéd spheres, and that to friends...
> For his bounty,
> There was no winter in't; an autumn 'twas
> That grew the more by reaping; his delights
> Were dolphin-like; they show'd his back above
> The element they lived in: in his livery
> Walked crowns and crownets; realms and islands were
> As plates dropped from his pocket.
>
> *Antony and Cleopatra*, v. ii. 83–92.

> And all such dull and heavy-witted worldlings as were never capable of the wit of a comedy, coming by report of them to his representations, have found that wit there that they never found in themselves, and have parted better witted than they came; feeling an edge of wit set upon them more than ever they dreamed they had brain to grind it on. So much and such savoured salt of wit is in his comedies, that they seem, for their height of pleasure, to be born in the sea that brought forth Venus.
>
> Publisher's preface to *Troilus and Cressida*, 1609.

SHAKESPEARE at thirty, then, was a light-hearted dramatic poet, who had succeeded in securing what all poets of that age strove to secure, the admiring patronage of a powerful circle of cultivated noblemen at court. For them he wrote his poems, and chiefly for them too, as I believe, he wrote his comedies, his early tragedies and histories. And though he wrote to please, he did so to please himself quite as much as his patrons; for he admired them as much as they admired him. Their tastes were his own, and the mutual admiration sprang from "the marriage of true minds".

68

He must have been a very fascinating person to meet. His manners, as we have seen, were charming, while in respect of looks and conversation a good tradition which comes from the son of one of his fellow-players pictures us "a handsome, well-shaped man, very good company, and of a very ready and pleasant smooth wit". A handsome poet with ready wit, a poet who is good company, a poet who can turn the laugh upon himself, who can class poets with lunatics and frantic lovers, who can write

> The poet's eye in a fine frenzy rolling,
> Doth glance from heaven to earth, from earth
> to heaven,

and then go on divinely

> And as imagination bodies forth
> The forms of things unknown, the poet's pen
> Turns them to shapes and gives to airy nothing
> A local habitation and a name—

such a poet was surely one of the most delightful companions the world has ever known. Every scrap of contemporary evidence points in this direction. There are stories, true or false, of unedifying escapades, but of his person the tide of epithets flows one way only: "gentle", "friendly", "civil", "brave" (that is, gallant), "dear-loved", and always affectionately "our Shakespeare" or "my Shakespeare", are the phrases that come to men's mind when they mention him. Jonson will fiercely criticise his art, but no sooner does he think of the artist than he cries "I did love the man this side idolatry as much as any".

Some moderns have conjured from all this an image of a shy effeminate creature, one who in actual life seemed to lack character and personality that he might the more readily absorb the life around him. Could Jonson have "loved" such a man? Could such a man have begotten Falstaff, or Toby Belch, or Mercutio, or Antony? Fuller, it is true, wrote forty years after his death, but when he declared "his genius generally was jocular, inclining him to festivity" the statement has the ring of truth. The man who created the comedies was a good "mixer" in companies of all sorts, and in merry-making as in other of life's occasions it is more blessed to give than to receive. The silent man is never popular and whatever else the man Shakespeare may have been he was certainly popular. Nor can there have been anything effeminate about him. He was no Tybalt, and despised the duelling fashion as new-fangled, but like other men of the time he wore steel at his side, and could draw if the occasion really warranted. A recent discovery at the Record Office shows us "a certain loose person of no reckoning or value", seeking to protect himself from we know not what just chastisement, by claiming from the Court of Queen's Bench legal security against Shakespeare and three others "for fear of death and mutilation of his limbs". Furthermore, he was a keen sportsman, as every reader of the plays and of Madden's delightful *Diary of Master William Silence* knows. The chase was a passion with him, like music. Wherever man's business was afoot, was it hunting or coursing in wood or field, taking a part in the prick-song after supper, or making one in a tavern over a cup of sack and sugar, his gay spirit would be there, in the forefront of the enterprise. It is surely a strange notion that poetry and full-blooded manhood cannot go together. Most of the great poets have been exceedingly virile, not excepting Keats who, until consumption gripped him, was a boxer and a walker.

Yet the five or six years we have now to consider, seemingly so auspicious and free from care, were not free from hard and continuous work. Even if his mind and hand went together, as Heminge and Condell declared, only incessant application at the desk can have produced a dozen plays like *The Merchant of Venice* and *Richard II*, the three Falstaff dramas, the three supreme lyrical comedies, *Henry V*, *Julius Caesar*, *Troilus and Cressida* and *Hamlet*, to say nothing about the revision of old material and such trifles as *King John*, in half that number of years. How did Shakespeare work? We do not know, though we may suspect. Certainly Ben Jonson's famous lines about him—

> Yet must I not give nature all: thy art,
> My gentle Shakespeare, must enjoy a part;
> For though the poet's matter nature be,
> His art doth give the fashion; and that he,
> Who casts to write a living line, must sweat
> (Such as thine are), and strike the second heat
> Upon the muses' anvil—turn the same
> (And himself with it) that he thinks to frame,
> Or for the laurel he may gain a scorn:
> For a good poet's made as well as born,
> And such wert thou—

71

will not do, being clearly inspired by refusal to believe that composition could come easier to Shakespeare than to himself. There is, however, another passage in Ben Jonson, describing an unnamed writer, which has always seemed to me as probably referring to Shakespeare, since it would explain so much in his plays; that fiery intensity, followed by periods of lassitude; that strange combination of the minutest care with culpable negligence; those loose ends, gaping flats and huddled finales, so that he seems to tire even of *Romeo and Juliet* in the last act. The passage occurs in the posthumous *Discoveries*, from which Jonson's praise of Shakespeare has already been quoted, and runs as follows:

Ease and relaxation are profitable to all studies. The mind is like a bow, the stronger by being unbent. But the temper in spirits is all, when to command a man's wit, when to favour it. I have known a man vehement on both sides; that knew no mean either to intermit his studies or call upon them again. When he hath set himself to writing, he would join night to day; press upon himself without release, not minding it till he fainted: and when he left off, resolve himself into all sports and looseness again; that it was almost a despair to draw him to his book: but once got to it, he grew stronger and more earnest by the ease. His whole powers were renewed: he would work out of himself what he desired, but with such excess as his study could not be ruled: he knew not how to dispose his own abilities or husband them, he was of that immoderate power against himself.

Nor when the periods of intermission came was the world one to be altogether at ease in. Fortune, as we have seen, had been kind, very kind; it had given him powerful and wealthy patrons, the best

72

company to write for in England, and a field without competitors. Yet in those days the greater the success, the more the peril. Shakespeare knew this well enough; was it not one of his own dramatic themes? "The primrose path", too, was a phrase often in his mind; it is found, in slightly varying forms, three times in his plays, and always in the Biblical sense, the sense of "the flowery way that leads to the broad gate and the great fire". Horrible examples of "mighty poets in their misery dead" who had trod that path were before him. Greene and Peele had come to destitution and a death by foul disease through excess and self-indulgence: Marlowe and Kyd had dared to meddle with matters of state and had been untimely cut off. No wonder he took care not to be drawn into the sink of debauchery which opened up at his doors whether he lodged in Shoreditch or on Bankside. He was "the more to be admired", we are told by the son of one of his fellow-actors, "that he was not a company keeper...he would not be debauched, and if invited to, writ he was in pain".

The other danger required even greater wariness, for to serve a patron was to be a party man; and, though in 1594 every star in the sky seemed auspicious for Essex, Southampton and their friends, at any moment fortune might turn her wheel and the whole glittering edifice of court favour come crashing to the ground. There was not only the dashing and violent Raleigh to reckon with; much more ominous were the cold, self-possessed figures of Burleigh and his crook-backed son, Robert Cecil.

Moreover, the leader of the faction, Essex himself, was already exhibiting an instability which augured ill for the future. What could a poor player do in such slippery circumstance? All we know for certain is that when the crash did come and the dust of it had cleared away, he was found, not indeed unchanged but apparently unharmed.

Of his escape I offer two explanations. First of all, however much he might owe to Southampton, however fervently he professed himself his servant, he held an independent position and had contracted obligations which both men acknowledged to have first claim upon him. He might lament in the *Sonnets* the irksomeness of his profession:—

> Alas, 'tis true I have gone here and there
> And made myself a motley to the view,
> Gored mine own thoughts, sold cheap what is most dear,
> Made old offences of affections new;

Or again,

> O, for my sake do you with Fortune chide,
> The guilty goddess of my harmful deeds,
> That did not better for my life provide
> Than public means which public manners breeds.

But such regrets remind his patron that there was business at the theatre which must be done; and just as he avoided drinking-bouts with boon companions by pleading toothache or headache, so he could always excuse himself from dancing attendance upon Southampton by urging that a play had to be finished or a rehearsal attended to, an excuse that the young earl with his love of the stage would readily accept. Nor was he under any financial necessity of courting patronage, once the theatres had righted themselves after the great plague of 1592–4. The player, with his share in a flourishing company and the special fees he received for furnishing them with play-books, was in a far more secure position than the professional writer like Nashe, or Donne, or even Ben Jonson, who could not live without a patron for any length of time. Further, he not only got his livelihood by writing and acting for a company, he did it for *the* company, for the servants of the Lord Chamberlain, who was himself responsible for all the entertainments given at court. Thus the writer for the Chamberlain Men held virtually an official position, which became actually one when, at James's accession, he and his fellows were made grooms of the chamber and given the style of "King's Men". His Lord Chamberlain's badge, therefore, was a breastplate, and his work for the company a fortress, behind which he could always retire with polite apologies not to be brushed aside, if dangerous courses were proposed. It was his clear duty so to do, since, as a member of a fellowship of players, he had no right to take action which might imperil the financial stability of his co-sharers, still less their personal safety.

And the second reason, as I believe, for his winning through, and bringing his fellows with him, was his own admirable circumspection. However he might yield himself to the frenzy of inspiration when the mood for composition was on him, he kept his head in the practical affairs of life. This

75

was due not to any cold and calculated policy of self-interest, such for instance as directed Bacon's steps in the same circumstances, but rather on the contrary to his large-hearted tolerance and universal sympathy, to what Keats called that "negative capability" of his which was the foundation and condition of all his art. He never commits himself deeply to a cause or to a point of view, whatever his affection or admiration for those who held it might be, because Life itself in all its infinite variety is far more interesting than any opinions, doctrines or points of view about it. No sooner, for example, had he captured London by *Venus and Adonis* than he turns to the "graver labour" of *The Rape of Lucrece*, as if to say "You thought I was that kind of man, but you were mistaken: I can sing the praises of Chastity with the best of them. Or rather, I am not to be labelled with moral labels at all: I am a poet, who chooses to make a study of Desire one day and of Chastity the next". Like his royal mistress he went forward by keeping his balance.

By 1594 or 1595 Shakespeare had won fame, chiefly for two very different things: for a command of lyrical verse, fluent and melodious in the poems, eager and passionate in *Romeo and Juliet*; and for his successful handling of comic drama, which might be witty or romantic or both combined. He had also attempted history plays, not so successfully. All three veins were now to be exploited to the full. We shall briefly consider each in turn, and as we do so we shall now and again have sight of a fourth. Save for *Romeo and Juliet* and *Richard II*, Shakespeare

76

has little commerce with the tragic muse for several years, but the indications are many that he had not forgotten her; and as he probed human character deeper, and came more and more to see life whole, he one day discovered that life and tragedy were the same.

Shakespeare did not easily come to character-making. At first the only kind he seemed to be able to endow with full humanity was comic character, especially comic character in low life. The living beings in *A Midsummer-Night's Dream* are the Mechanicals, and in *The Two Gentlemen* Lance. Marlowe had rejected "such conceits as clownage keeps in pay"; Shakespeare made them the headstone of his corner. The old type of stage-clown had been contemptible enough no doubt; the jests of the famous Tarlton that have come down to us are mere flimflam. Yet Shakespeare saw its possibilities and gave it a new and glorious lease of life by humanising it and planting it once more in English soil. Under his hands the conventional buffoon becomes an English yokel. In *The Two Gentlemen* he gives us a representative of both types, old and new, Speed and Lance. Was he testing his audience to discover which had their suffrage? If so, the issue is not in doubt; for Lance became the father of a long line; of Bottom, the Dromios, Costard, Lancelot Gobbo, to name but a handful of them, while Bottom's self-description, "a tender ass", will serve as a label for the whole species. But Shakespeare did more than humanise; he, as ever, subtilised. As his hand grew more practised, his human clown developed along

77

two lines, which we may call "the dry clown" and "the sly clown"; the former a butt to be laughed at, an English clod untroubled with a spark, the latter a simpleton who "uses his folly like a stalking-horse and under the presentation of that shoots his wit". Neither sort of fool talks rubbish, be it observed, though perplexed editors have often supposed so: the one blunders or wanders most ludicrously, the other quibbles or equivocates with exquisite finesse. Thus Shakespeare made his clowns worthy the attention of the judicious, of a South-ampton or a Ben Jonson. William and Touchstone in *As You Like It* furnish examples of both kinds: and the mention of Touchstone shows to what lengths Shakespeare carried the type first created in Lance. It is pretty certain too that the full development had to wait until he found a comic actor capable of interpreting it. The departure of William Kempe from his company about 1599, and the coming of Robert Armin meant much to Shakespeare; it made Feste and the Fool in *King Lear* possible.

The dry fool had his female counterpart in those garrulous old women, of whom the Nurse in *Romeo and Juliet* is the first, though Mistress Quickly is the supreme instance. As Bagehot, one of the best of Shakespearian critics, remarks, Shakespeare "would never have interrupted Mistress Quickly; he saw that her mind was going to and fro over the subject, he saw that it was coming right, and this was enough for him".

Among his creatures of the upper class, it was once again the comic characters which first seemed fully flesh and blood, the most successful for some reason in the early plays being forceful, bluff, yet vivacious and humorous soldier-men. Perhaps Shakespeare knew someone of this type and had an admiration for him; perhaps Burbadge was specially happy in "creating" such parts. At all events, Mercutio in *Romeo and Juliet*, the Bastard in *King John*, and Berowne in *Love's Labour's Lost* are all from the same mould, and each is the most intensely realised character in the play he belongs to. Benedick in *Much Ado* is a later incarnation of the same spirit, while in very different fashions Petruchio of *The Shrew* and King Harry the Fifth himself owe something to it.

Long before he reached *Much Ado* and *Henry V*, however, Shakespeare was able to throw off play after play containing whole galleries of characters far more real than most of the people one encounters in life. And as the characters came flocking to him, blank verse, which had once cramped his hand like a new glove, became as flexible as a second skin, a perfect medium for the multitude of voices whispering at his ear and demanding expression.

The earliest play in which Shakespeare found himself in the fullest sense was, I think, *The Merchant of Venice*, a new departure for him in more ways than one. How tragic a misfortune that this great play has been staled and hackneyed for so many modern readers by the treadmill methods of the class-room, where the dull brain of the pedagogic presenter perplexes and retards! It is a play with three magnificent scenes, which can only be fully apprehended in the traffic of the stage: the casket scene, the trial scene, and the last and loveliest scene of all at Belmont. It is a play of wonderful poetry, most wonderful perhaps in the finale, but reaching greater heights of intensity in Shylock's mouth. And it is a play in which Shakespeare makes what was a forward leap in his grasp of character. How great the leap was, is best understood if we remember that it was probably, at any rate in its first draft, the next play he took in hand after *Love's Labour's Lost*. It has neither a Berowne nor a Mercutio, but the trio, Antonio, Bassanio and Gratiano, make a stronger stage-group than anything Shakespeare had accomplished so far, while when we turn to the women we find in Portia and Nerissa the earliest of his ladies to be fully human. Lancelot too, admirably set off by old Gobbo, is far the best thing in clowns up to now. And in Shylock we have something entirely new and very pregnant for the future.

Shakespeare created three characters, of the first order, which have given rise to serious perplexity and difference of opinion among critics: Shylock, Hamlet, and Cleopatra. The difficulty is the same with all: the character is at once so subtly conceived and presented so completely in the full human round that it escapes a grasp accustomed to conventional stage figures and one-sided types. Shylock, the earliest and simplest problem of the three, gives the clue to the others. Two views are current about him: one, very popular since the time of Irving, of a great tragic figure, representative of the suffering Hebrew race throughout history and expressing the indignation and the aspirations of oppressed peoples and races throughout the world; the other, traditional on the stage until at any rate the time of Charles Kean, of a comic character, of a devil in the likeness of an old Jew, a crafty bloodthirsty villain, crying out for revenge upon a decent Christian gentleman, and—at the last moment—hoist with his own petar. The apparent antinomy may be resolved in simple fashion. Shakespeare intended both Shylocks. He inherited a Jew play upon which he constructed *The Merchant*, and he developed the character he found therein. He loaded the dice still more heavily against him; he made him more bloodthirsty than before; he wrote the Tubal scene which must have seemed exquisitely ludicrous to most of his audience. Yet the other Shylock was also Shakespeare's from the start, the conscious product of his genius, deliberately set forth for the judicious to ponder. In a word, Shylock is the first unmistakable example of what may be called Shakespeare's tragic balance, the balance between pitiless observation and divine compassion and understanding. He hides nothing. He shows us everything of Shylock's meanness, cunning and cruelty—vices which he himself detested above all vices—and notwithstanding he compels the best of us, and the best in us, to cry out with Heine's "fair Briton" upon the Jew's exit, "By heaven, the man is wronged!"

This is the quality that makes Shakespeare one of the great moral forces of the world, a human saviour and redeemer. "The great secret of morals is Love", Shelley writes, "or a going out of our own nature, and an identification of ourselves with the beautiful which exists in thought, action, or person, not our own. A man to be greatly good must imagine intensely and comprehensively...the pains and pleasures of his species must become his own." Shakespeare is even more "greatly good" than Shelley suggests is possible; for he can identify himself with what he thought ugly and detestable, knocking all the time at our heart for pity and awe. No one but Dostoieffsky among the moderns can touch him here.

Shakespeare, then, of set purpose undertook to civilise this old play. But in so doing he was not working only under poetic inspiration. Indeed, the full implications of the creation of Shylock for his dramatic art came, I think, as a discovery even to himself. What set him first thinking about Jews was an event in real life, *the* event, in fact, during the early months of 1594 when he was first drafting the play. In February of that year a certain Dr Lopez, the royal physician and a Portuguese Jew, was put on trial at the Guildhall on the charge of attempting to poison the Queen. The whole affair created a great deal of public excitement and anti-semitic feeling ran high in London. It seems doubtful, to say the least of it, whether Lopez was guilty, and the Queen apparently believed him innocent. But the feet of the Earl of Essex were swift to shed blood. He owed the old physician a grudge; moreover he regarded the discovery of the plot as a triumph for the new secret service department he had just set up in rivalry to that belonging to the Cecils, who, now Raleigh was out of the way, alone stood between him and power. He was the main instigator of the process, and himself presided over the judicial proceedings at the Guildhall, like the Duke in the play, with the city fathers as his attendant magnificoes. Conviction followed; the reluctant Elizabeth was at last induced to sign the death-warrant; and the execution took place at Tyburn, on June 7, vast crowds, to a man hostile to the wretched victim, attending the hideous spectacle of hanging, drawing and quartering.

A passage in *The Merchant* comparing Shylock with a wolf "hanged for human slaughter" clearly points to Lopez whose name, often spelt "Lopus", would of course suggest "Wolf". I do not suppose that Shylock was in any sense a portrait of the royal physician; but it is certain that the play reflects in the mirror of dramatic art the "body of the time" which saw Lopez done to death. The trial scene was no doubt highly popular with the anti-semitic generality who found in Gratiano's attitude a fine and manly expression of their own feelings. But the figure of Shylock was also, I am convinced, intended to appeal to the compassion of Essex and other judicious spectators. And this is not all; for *The Merchant* contains the famous hymn in praise of Christian Mercy, a hymn worthy to be set beside that of St Paul in praise of Christian Love. I say "Christian Mercy" because it is based upon the Lord's Prayer and the Christian doctrine of salvation, and as such is most inappropriately addressed to a Jew. My belief is that Shakespeare is here speaking through Portia's mouth to the Christians in his audience, and especially to the "Duke". Certainly the reference in the speech to crowns, sceptres and thrones, which are once again pointless for Shylock, would sound gratefully in the ear of the Queen's favourite, who in secret cherished hopes of succeeding her. The appeal is subtle, discreet, entirely non-committal; and it failed. But Shakespeare could not see the bosom friend of his friend, whom he admired and to whom he owed much, "grow guilty of detested crimes...for fame's sake, for praise, an outward part", without doing what a dramatist could to compel him to bethink himself. This was by no means the last occasion on which he was to hold up the mirror to Essex.

Technically the character of Shylock was a great advance on anything Shakespeare had before attempted. He did not, however, follow it up at once by a second experiment of the same kind. Rather, he occupied himself for most of the remaining years of the sixteenth century with a character-problem of another nature. Shylock, created in two planes of vision as it were, is a marvel of penetration; but he is static, he does not develop. And what interests Shakespeare most at this time is character development. The ordinary type of static character, such as the Bastard in *King John*, Hotspur, Fluellen, Falstaff himself and his followers, together with all the jolly throng in *The Merry Wives*, no longer gave him the least trouble. He now set himself to discover the trick of making characters grow. Attempts come quite early. Proteus—the name is significant —was one, but a failure; and the botched finale of *The Two Gentlemen* is perhaps an endeavour to cut through a hopeless tangle. A far more successful experiment is the study of King Richard II, from the technical point of view almost as interesting as Shylock, and belonging to the same period. Richard has often been described as an immature Hamlet, and there are many likenesses. But if we are thinking of Shakespeare's progress in dramatic art, he is better regarded as an early Lear; for like Lear he begins as an impossible and capricious tyrant, and engages our sympathy more and more as Fate rains blow upon blow at his devoted and anointed head. Yet there is a great difference in the quality of our sympathy. What we feel for Richard is called forth entirely by the pathos of his situation and most of all by the fact that he is a *king* humbled to the dust by the results of his own folly. What we feel for Lear has all this, but how tremendously much more! Richard does not develop spiritually at all: Lear grows to heights of tragic grandeur which for ever enlarge the limits of spiritual possibility.

Richard II, then, though an interesting attempt, which will always fascinate the world by its sheer poetic beauty, was not a true success. Shakespeare next tried a new kind of development altogether. Instead of a prince who, beginning in the full flush of power which he misused, was stripped of his regalia piece by piece, he made a dramatic study of Prince Hal, an heir to the throne, who, beginning as a frivolous madcap despised by all serious persons, his father included, should become through the education of responsibility the ideal monarch. But this experiment is no more successful than the other. Prince Hal and King Henry V are different persons: the passage from one to the other is not by a process of growth but by theatrical legerdemain. It is usually supposed by critics that Falstaff is responsible for this miscarriage. On the contrary, Falstaff is the *deus ex machina* who saves the situation. Prince Hal, if we neglect his soliloquies, is a rounded whole; King Henry V is equally consistent and intelligible; but Shakespeare is forced to conceal the yawning gap between the two by that mountain of flesh he called Falstaff.

Shakespeare had not yet learnt how to make characters develop; he was not to understand spiritual growth until he had experienced it in himself.

This excursion into Shakespeare's education in the art of character-making has brought us up alongside of the four-staged pageant of his later English histories, which beginning with *Richard II* continues with the two parts of *Henry IV* and culminates in the dramatic epic of Agincourt, *Henry V*. The two main interests of the series are politics and Falstaff. They are attached however by the slenderest links; and I make no apology for considering them separately, and taking Falstaff first, together with the three comedies, *Much Ado*, *As You Like It*, and *Twelfth Night*, which belong to approximately the same period of production.

Sir John Falstaff, at any rate as we now know him,

first saw light during the happiest episode of Elizabeth's reign, the years 1597–8, when the three chief figures at her court, Essex, Raleigh and Cecil, were for once in accord and all London was given up to gaiety; while the Peace of Vervins between France and Spain and the death of England's inveterate foe, Philip II, both occurring in 1598, seemed to proclaim "olives of endless age". It was an auspicious hour for the birth of one of the greatest benefactors of the human race.

A long-faced fellow once taxed me with my reverence for Sir John's memory, and asked whether I realised the man was a filthy old ruffian, physically repulsive, disorderly in garb, in habits, in morals; in fact, not to put too fine a point upon it, a liar, a sot, a coward, and a whoremonger. I could not deny the accusations; there was too much support in the text for every one of them. How then do we come to be bewitched with the rogue's company? What medicines have we drunk to make us love him? The magic Shakespeare employs here as elsewhere is his poetic imagination; Falstaff is his greatest comic poem.

There is a passage in Rupert Brooke's *Memoir* which helps us to understand how the fat knight came into existence. Brooke is explaining to Keeling what it feels like to be a poet:

It consists in just looking at people and things as themselves—neither as useful nor moral nor ugly nor anything else; but just as being. At least that's a philosophical description of it. What happens is that I suddenly feel the extraordinary value and importance of everything I meet, and almost everything I see...I roam about places—

yesterday I did it even in Birmingham!—and sit in trains and see the essential glory and beauty of all the people I meet. I can watch a dirty middle-aged tradesman in a railway-carriage for hours, and love every dirty greasy sulky wrinkle in his weak chin and every button on his spotted unclean waistcoat. I know their states of mind are bad. But I'm so much occupied with their being there at all, that I don't have time to think of that. I tell you that a Birmingham gouty Tariff Reform fifth-rate business man is splendid and immortal and desirable.

That is the kind of mood in which Shakespeare created Falstaff; only he not merely saw that this filthy old ruffian was splendid and immortal and desirable, he made the world see it for all time by enduing him with such gaiety of spirit, such nimbleness of wit, such a varied flow of imagery, such perfect poise and self-assurance, and above all such magnificent vitality, that he has become a kind of god in the mythology of modern man, a god who does for our imaginations much what Silenus did for those of the ancients. Falstaff is, I say, essentially a poetic creation; he is a thing of beauty, even if "he hath a monstrous beauty, like the hindquarters of an elephant". The perpetual reflexions upon his bulk, of which we never grow weary, keep it ever before our minds, until it becomes a symbol of the enlargement and enfranchisement which he bestows upon us. For though he speaks of levers as necessary to lift him up again being down, we believe him in that no more than when he protests that he has "more flesh than another man and therefore more frailty". We know that fat belly, so far from dragging him earthwards, bears him hither and thither like a balloon, at the slightest whim or desire. He is an emancipated spirit, free of all the conventions, codes and moral ties that enwrap us. They are no doubt necessary, as necessary to life in a civilised community as clothes. Yet just because we can never be rid of them, it is extraordinarily exhilarating to contemplate a being who is; a being without shame, without principles, without even a sense of decency, who nevertheless manages to preserve our respect, to win our admiration.

What we chiefly admire him for is his abounding vitality. Falstaff is more than man; he is, like all great mythological figures, the incarnation of a principle of the universe. He is the Joy of Life, exuberant, intoxicating, irrepressible, the joy which in its particular form of Desire Shakespeare had already hymned in *Venus and Adonis*. Falstaff, to use the words of a contemporary quoted at the head of this chapter, was "born in the sea that brought forth Venus". The name of the sea is Poetry.

The success of Falstaff in 1597 was immense and instantaneous. When Lindrum made his record break the other day, it is said that the excitement was so great that all pipes went out in the hands and mouths of those who watched; when Falstaff "came on", we are told, an unwonted hush fell upon the theatre—the groundlings forgot to crack their nuts! A second part of *Henry IV* was called for. Not content with that the Queen commanded the production of yet a third play, this time showing Falstaff a thrall of the fair sex. The tun of flesh had become a national event. Shakespeare complied

89

with the royal order by producing *The Merry Wives*, according to a credible tradition, within a fortnight. What tradition does not tell us, though modern research has revealed it, is that the feat was accomplished by refurbishing an old play, previously handled, probably by Shakespeare himself, about 1593, and perhaps going further back still. The reshaped *Wives* is highly entertaining, one of the jolliest and most rollicking of all Shakespeare's comedies; its hero, or villain, is not, however, Sir John of Eastcheap, but a Windsor cousin of his with the same name. After this it was clear that Shakespeare must do something if he was not to be condemned to writing Falstaff plays for the rest of his life. He took the only course possible, and killed the fat man off at the beginning of *Henry V*.

Yet even so "the sea that brought forth Venus" was not exhausted of prodigies, and during the final years of the century London witnessed the subtlest, wittiest, and most exquisite of all the comedies. *Much Ado* is the earliest, in which Shakespeare harks back to the "sets of wit well played" between a bluff soldier-man and a "mocking wench", first exploited in *Love's Labour's Lost*; though never had the steel been so bright or the thrust and parry so rapid as between Benedick and Beatrice. There followed *As You Like It*, a pastoral tapestry with shepherds and shepherdesses, an exiled Duke in his woodland court, disguised princesses, a melancholy man and a fool, all "fleeting the time carelessly as they did in the golden world"; which nevertheless very shrewdly hits off the prevailing Arcadian fashion. Last and best came *Twelfth Night*, which for sheer lightness of touch goes as far as even Shakespeare can reach, blending music and revelry, realism and romance, the wittiest prose and the most ravishing poetry.

Twelfth Night is Shakespeare's farewell to comedy for many years. It is fitting that the earliest recorded performance should have been at a feast in the Middle Temple, since this marks the fact that from beginning to end the comedies and histories were composed for audiences of young men. It is *Twelfth Night* also which provides youth with its eternal retort to the cooling blood of age: "Dost think, because thou art virtuous, there shall be no more cakes and ale?"

HISTORY AND POLITICS

For to the king God hath his office lent
Of dread of justice, power and command,
Hath bid him rule and willed you to obey;
And to add ampler majesty to this,
He hath not only lent the king his figure,
His throne and sword, but given him his own name,
Calls him a god on earth. What do you, then,
Rising 'gainst him that God himself installs
But rise 'gainst God? What do you to your souls
In doing this?

Shakespeare's addition to *Sir Thomas More*.

SIDE by side with the luxuriant growth of comedy we have been considering, a growth ever putting forth fresh blossom, each more entrancing than the last, there took root and flourished a very different interest in the mind of Shakespeare, a concern for politics, or rather for the dramatic possibilities of political life.

The political philosophy—if that be not too large a term—of Shakespeare's histories is simple enough. Social stability, in the form of a hierarchy of rank or degree, crowned by the monarchy, was, as we have seen, the condition of Elizabethan political thought. In this system the monarchy was all important, and the body politic hung suspended as it were from the throne as the universe itself hung from the floor of heaven. Everything then in literal truth *depended* upon the person of the King. If he was wise, of strong character, and with a firm policy, the balance of the commonwealth was preserved; if he was weak, capricious or evil, the balance was disturbed, lesser lights in the state-heaven started from their spheres in pursuit of personal ambition; and if the worst befell Chaos ensued. Shakespeare had been led to brood over such a chaos in the early days of his career. How large a share he had in the writing of the *Henry VI* trilogy is a matter of dispute, but during the years 1590 to 1594 he was certainly handling plays which depicted England torn asunder by civil strife, a prey to foreign invasion, arriving at that last stage of dissolution when father lifted hand against son, son against father, and the lowest elements of the populace rose—as if

> the bounded waters
> Should lift their bosoms higher than the shores,
> And make a sop of all this solid globe—

with Jack Cade and his rabble to lead them.

If the royal house could provide no strong man to save the country from this terrible fate, one of two things might happen: either chaos might itself give birth to some monstrous tyranny such as that depicted in *Richard III*, or one of the planetary nobles, stronger and better than the rest, might usurp the throne and found a new line of kings. This second alternative is the theme of *Richard II*. Bolingbroke was necessary: he saved England from chaos by imposing his will upon her; but in doing so, he sinned. Richard for all his weakness and instability was the Lord's anointed. In lifting up his hand against him, Bolingbroke had in effect struck at God himself; and Richard because of "the divinity that doth hedge a king", assumes at the end of his tragedy the character of the sacrificial victim, the god slain upon the altar, which we moderns can only begin to understand by reading a book like Sir James Frazer's *Golden Bough*. The usurper himself is conscious of his sin, and seeks to expiate it by undertaking a crusade in the Holy Land. Other members of the state are conscious of it also, for a weak title is only less dangerous to stability than a weak character; and the political theme of the two parts of *Henry IV* is the disorder that may fall upon the state through this weakness. The rebels are of course the great barons, who feel themselves peers of the man they have set upon the throne and resent his assumed authority; and Hotspur is the chief spokesman of their point of view. But Shakespeare lived at a time when men were becoming very conscious that above the interests of nobles, however brilliant and attractive, above the claims of "honour" and legality, even above the throne itself, there was the cause of

> This happy breed of men, this little world,
> This precious stone set in the silver sea...
> This blessed plot, this earth, this realm, this England.

Now the only security for England against internal strife and the "envy of less happier lands" was a king who, with divine right on his side, that is to say, a clear title to the throne, and with the sceptre firmly in his grasp, could identify himself fully with his people, could be the leader of a united England, a harmonious common weal, in which the noble, the merchant, the yeoman and the peasant, worked together for the good of the whole. The England of Elizabeth was sufficiently near to this happy consummation for men to dream of its complete fulfilment. Shakespeare expresses this dream in his *Henry V*, in which the whole nation, even the whole British Isles, under the ideal king realise themselves and their unity in the only way at that time considered possible, a victorious campaign against a foreign enemy. Some moderns find *Henry V* uninteresting and even forced. I saw it played at Stratford in the first week of the Great War, and shall never forget the excitement of those three hours. The epic drama of Agincourt matched the mood of the time (when Rupert Brooke was writing his sonnet on *The Soldier*), so exactly that it might have been written expressly for it. That mood has passed for us survivors, who sit and rub our sores amid the dust and ashes of the world conflagration. But the mood has been, may be again, and was certainly the mood of Englishmen in 1599, the last and crowning year of the greatest decade of English history, which began with the defeat of the Spanish Armada and ended with the return of a disgraced Essex from the fatal mists of Ireland.

Such was the historical pageant and the political philosophy set forth by Shakespeare on the London stage between the years 1590 and 1599. Popular interest in history had been greatly stimulated by the events of 1588, and shortly afterwards an expeditionary force was dispatched to France to help Henry of Navarre against the Catholic League, and remained on French soil from 1591 to 1593. The Earl of Essex was for a time in command; he was later leader of the brilliant naval raid upon Cadiz in

1596, and of the less successful Island Voyage of the following year. Essex was, in fact, "the centre and focus of national feeling, the darling hope of all who looked to have England a power on the seas and the champion of the Protestant cause in Europe". And behind Essex stood Southampton, his close friend, the sharer in all his counsels, the fellow dreamer of his dreams. I find it impossible to doubt that Southampton's poet had Essex in mind while writing these historical plays or that they were written primarily for "the judicious" of the Essex circle. Henry V is not of course, let me guard myself once again, a portrait of Essex; he was created as an appeal to Essex to become that kind of man, to perform that kind of work for England. In 1599, when the play was written, Elizabeth was sixty-six years old, and had no heir. Essex, then thirty-two, was her cousin; he was the most popular man in England, he was a brilliant and engaging personality; what other Englishman had a better chance of succeeding her? All he had to do was to secure her "voice" before she died, and the crown was his.

All four plays of the series have points of contact with Essex. Essex like Prince Hal had been a scapegrace in his early days; his intrigues with ladies at court were notorious; he was fond of low life and boon companions. In 1596, he suddenly, like Prince Hal, became a reformed character, and took for a time to devotion and pious exercises. The figure of Fluellen in *Henry V*, again, is a careful and unmistakable portrait—a real portrait—of Sir Roger Williams, the Welsh soldier who had accompanied

Essex during the French campaign of 1592 and had died, tended by Essex to the last, in 1595. That this old friend should reappear in a stage-representation of Agincourt four years later is strong evidence that the play was intended to be associated with the hope of England. Lastly, as every one knows, Essex is referred to personally in one of the choruses of the play. But to explain this and the strange link between *Richard II* and the fortunes of the earl, a brief account must be given of the events of 1598–1601.

Essex, generous and impetuous one minute, moody and suspicious the next, was wax in the hands of skilful intriguers like Cecil who, towards the end of 1598, finding the favourite's power at court and his popularity in the country growing too strong, manœuvred him into demanding for himself the most dangerous post in Elizabeth's service, the Lord-deputyship of Ireland, where he was required to crush the rebellion of Tyrone, who had won a resounding victory over the English on August 14 at Armagh. He had no sooner been appointed than he realised he had been trapped, and delayed his departure as long as possible. But putting-off and putting-off was part of his nature. And though he eventually left England on March 27, 1599, with Southampton as his Master of Horse and an army large enough in competent hands to effect all that was required, a strange malaise seemed to fall upon him. Month after month passed with nothing done; and when at last an angry command reached him from Elizabeth, he actually dallied for a while with the idea of marching on London at the head of his army instead of attacking Tyrone. On August 25 however he turned against the Irish. But only to parley, not to fight, and to concede a truce, the advantages of which were all on their side. Then, frightened of his action and conscious of failure, he suddenly determined to throw himself upon the Queen's mercy; took horse with a handful of followers; and arrived at Nonsuch Palace early on September 28, to burst into Elizabeth's chamber before she was fully dressed.

The rest of the story must be briefly told. The day after his arrival he found himself a prisoner in the house of the Lord Keeper whence he was only released on June 5, 1600, after making his submission in full council. He was free; but he was also a ruined man, since the Queen had deprived him of a monopoly from which he drew his income. Months of sullen discontent followed, his friends urging him to act and seize the person of the aged Queen, to preserve her from his enemies and hers. At last on February 8, 1601, he made a gambler's throw, and marched into the city appealing to all to rise in his favour. Not a soul responded; the whole thing was a miserable fiasco; Essex was sent to the Tower, tried on February 19, with Southampton, for high treason and executed on February 25, his friend being spared on the ground of youth. To the horror of all decent spirits, Francis Bacon, who owed him more than any of his other followers, appeared in the trial as his chief accuser and the architect of his ruin.

Shakespeare's attitude and feelings throughout

these tense months, followed by so terrible a cat-astrophe, can only be guessed at. Scholars of the "impersonal" school would say they should not be guessed at. Yet if his plays exhibit the very "body of the time, its form and pressure", it ought to be possible to catch some reflexion in them of the doings in London during 1599 to 1601. No one doubts, at any rate, that *Henry V* has relevance to the Irish campaigns, since Shakespeare tells us so him-self in the chorus to Act v, which, after describing the return to England of Henry, proceeds

> But now behold,
> In the quick forge and working-house of thought,
> How London doth pour out her citizens!—
> The mayor, and all his brethren, in best sort,
> Like to the senators of antique Rome,
> With the plebeians swarming at their heels,
> Go forth and fetch their conquering Caesar in:
> As by a lower but loving likelihood,
> Were now the general of our gracious empress,
> As in good time he may, from Ireland, coming,
> Bringing rebellion broached upon his sword,
> How many would the peaceful city quit,
> To welcome him! much more, and much more cause,
> Did they this Harry.

Some have believed that the play, which must have followed hard upon *Henry IV* (pt. ii) and *The Merry Wives*, was already on the stage in the winter of 1598–99. If so, it may have been seen, perhaps privately, by Essex and Southampton before their departure; and the lines quoted may have been added in the early summer of 1599 when Shake-speare's company began playing at the new-built

99   7-2

Globe, and when, as is generally supposed, *Henry V*
was given as one of its earliest pieces.

But if Shakespeare sent Essex off with *Henry V* he
greeted him on his return with *Julius Caesar*, the first
recorded performance of which was September 21,
a week before the disgraced general burst, mud-
stained and booted, into the Queen's bedroom. The
play must, of course, have been taken in hand soon
after *Henry V* was finished. But Shakespeare knew
his Essex, and news of his extraordinary conduct of
affairs would be reaching London by midsummer;
while Lytton Strachey is right, I think, in detecting
a note of anxiety even in the lines just quoted from
Henry V. Whether Shakespeare acted upon knowledge or was inspired by

> the prophetic soul
> Of the wide world dreaming on things to come,

certainly he could have furnished no more prescient
or more ominous prelude to the events of the next
sixteen months than this play of dark conspiracy
and of noble idealism brought to nought. Like *The
Merchant of Venice*, *Julius Caesar* was a play from which
Essex might have learnt much had he been
teachable.

In the spring of 1598 the poet Chapman had issued
the first instalment of his translation of Homer's *Iliad*
which he dedicated "To the most honoured now
living instance of the Achilleian virtues eternized
by divine Homer, the Earl of Essex". Chapman
was an old antagonist of Shakespeare's; he is
laughed at in *Love's Labour's Lost* and is probably

referred to in the *Sonnets* as the rival poet suing for Southampton's patronage. Anyhow, it is tolerably certain that in *Troilus and Cressida* Shakespeare is to some extent ridiculing the translation of 1598; and Dr Harrison has recently propounded the theory that, adopting the parallel in Chapman's dedication, Shakespeare intended the Achilles of his play to suggest Essex to the private audience before which it was given, an audience which he takes to have been composed of Essex's opponents. My view is different. Written, I think, in those last bitter months of 1600 when Essex moped and sulked, and would or could do nothing, *Troilus and Cressida* was Shakespeare's courageous, almost savage, attempt to goad the earl into action. "This fellow Chapman likens your lordship to Achilles", he said in effect; "let me show you Achilles in the dramatic mirror; does the comparison flatter you?" It was bitter medicine, but

> diseases desperate grown
> By desperate appliance are relieved,
> Or not at all,

and by the latter part of 1600 the friends of Essex were at their wits' end. Yet I cannot believe for a moment that Shakespeare was recommending rebellion. On the contrary, the whole point of the play is the paralysis of the Greeks owing to disunion in the camp and to Achilles' refusal to go out to battle. For what purpose too was the magnificent speech on "degree" written except to stamp rebellion as a sin against the universal order of things? Surely the moral was plain: give up sulking, make terms with your Prince, think of England first. There were two opinions among Essex's friends: one urged him to seize the crown at once by force; the other pointed out that if he only waited, and wisely became friends with the old Queen, the crown would fall into his lap. Shakespeare's inclination to the latter view cannot be doubted.

But Essex was unteachable, and how much he, or some of his followers, misunderstood Shakespeare and his point of view may be seen from the strange incident of the playing of *Richard II* on the eve of the rebellion. History judges its characters by the accomplished fact, and Elizabeth shines at us across the centuries like some steel-built personality of tenacity and purpose. To her contemporaries, exasperated by her vacillations, she appeared the very reverse, and there is ample evidence that she was frequently compared with Richard II, and was even herself conscious that such comparisons were made. With this in mind members of the Essex party on February 7, the day before the rising, induced Shakespeare's company to give a performance of *Richard II* at the Globe Theatre, with a view to inciting the people against the Queen and showing them that sovereigns had been deposed and might be again. The play was given, and the deposition scene in particular was greeted with loud applause by friends of Essex in the audience. It is at once difficult to see how Shakespeare escaped being mixed up in all this, and impossible to believe that he approved of it. At the subsequent trial, the whole story came out, and for a time things looked black for the Globe and its company. Yet in the end they took no hurt, and are even found playing before the Queen on February 24th, the eve of Essex's death. How this happened history does not tell us, but if the Lord Chamberlain was a sensible man, a few words of explanation from the author of the play as to its exact tenour and purport should have placed matters in a proper light.

The tragedy of Essex was a tragedy of character. Even right up to the last he might have saved the situation. Elizabeth loved the man, and did all she could for him until matters became impossible. But for his extraordinary moodiness, procrastination, violent outbursts of temper, indecision of purpose, and general emotional instability, which seemed to grow upon him and at times to verge upon madness, he might have triumphed over Tyrone, and perhaps have ascended the throne. Furthermore, as we have seen, he could be implacably cruel, and was in his earlier days a ruthless woman-hunter. Yet he possessed most attractive qualities. He was generous to a fault, the soul of loyalty to his friends, open and frank in manner, ever gracious and kindly to dependents, a man of wide cultural interests, a poet of some distinction, a brilliant conversationalist, capable of heartfelt and sincere piety, a devoted husband, and, though no general, a rashly brave soldier. He seemed a bundle of contradictions, to explain which baffled even the subtlest of his contemporaries.

It was inevitable that such an enigmatic figure, so close to him, and while alive so portentous for the future of the whole state, should fascinate the greatest imagination of the age. And if in the example of Henry V he showed "virtue her own feature" and in the warning of Achilles he showed "scorn her own image", I believe, as many other writers have done, that in the central figure of yet a third play he attempted a really detailed reflexion of the inner Essex. I mean Hamlet, Prince of Denmark; and I say "the inner Essex" because Hamlet is not Essex, he is Shakespeare's effort to understand Essex, to understand him as a dramatist, not as a psychologist. Shakespeare does not "explain" Hamlet (he leaves his critics to do that!), he reveals him.

Hamlet the play goes back a long way, and was in some form or other being acted by Shakespeare's company as early as 1594. Shakespeare himself had probably handled it by 1598, since there is a reference to his *Hamlet* in that year or soon after, and since the figure of Polonius is almost without doubt intended as a caricature of Burleigh, who died on August 4, 1598. On the other hand, it is certain that the text as we now have it dates from after the death of Essex because the passage about the "little eyases that cry out in the top of question" in Act II is a reference to the Quarrel of the Theatres, begun by Ben Jonson (then writing plays for the Children of the Chapel) into which the Chamberlain Men were not drawn until well on in 1601. It looks therefore as if Shakespeare had in Essex's lifetime

set him up a glass
Where he might see the inmost part of him.

If so, we may suppose that the touches added in

1601 give Shakespeare's final thoughts of a man at once very dear to him and very clearly judged, a man full of faults and of much nobility, but with faults softened (not concealed) by the tragic atmosphere of his piteous end, in the flower of his years, and when England needed him most.

The more one studies the character of the ill-starred Essex, the more remarkable Shakespeare's portraiture becomes. Everything is there: his courtesy, his kindness to inferiors, his intellectual virtues, his passion for drama, his interest in spiritualism, his open and free nature, his nobility of bearing, his piety, his bravery, his genius for friendship, his brilliant wit, his love of field-sports, of hawking and horsemanship; and, on the other side, his moods of profound melancholy, his touch of insanity, his dangerous impetuosity, his frequent talk of suicide, his coarseness, his brutality and callousness to women, his ruthlessness towards those he hated, his theatricality, and above all his complete inability to think out a continuous line of action. Essex in Ireland during 1599, frittering away a summer and an army; when forced to act, debating whether to march on Elizabeth or Tyrone; and lastly, having signed the ignominious truce, suddenly posting to England and dashing into the Queen's bedroom, behaves exactly as Hamlet would have acted under the same conditions. Hamlet, unable to accomplish his design, a design long premeditated, necessary for him, for his mother's honour, for his father's honour, for the whole state of Denmark, and yet always ready to act upon impulse, to test his uncle with a play which will reveal his own hand, to kill an unknown man behind a curtain, to get clear of his guards and leave them to incur the death devised for him, to fall into the trap about the duel, simply acts as Essex would have acted had he lived at Elsinore. Even some of the incidents of the story are the same. For instance, in Horatio's final prayer

> And flights of angels sing thee to thy rest,

which grates upon our religious sensibility, we have, I think, an echo of the twice repeated prayer of Essex on the scaffold that God should send his angels to convey his soul to the joys of Heaven.

And Hamlet's mystery? Hamlet's mystery is the mystery of Essex. Shakespeare does not solve it; he could not if he would. Why the "darling of England" should have cast away the greatest opportunities that ever fell to an Elizabethan, why

> The courtier's, soldier's, scholar's, eye, tongue, sword;
> The expectancy and rose of the fair state,
> The glass of fashion and the mould of form,
> The observed of all observers,

should have come to the block, no one could tell. But one thing was acknowledged by all, even by Essex himself in the Tower, that for all Cecil's cunning, Raleigh's hatred, and Bacon's treachery, the heart of the mystery was the heart of Essex. Such was the verdict of contemporaries, of history, and such is the moral of *Hamlet*. Shakespeare was obliged, and was content to be obliged, to etch in the man and his mystery by a thousand loving and delicate touches of dramatic art, and leave it for the admiration and perplexity of those who came after.

The reader must not misunderstand me. There is of course much more, an infinite deal more, in *Hamlet* than this, for *Hamlet* has more facets than any other jewel in Shakespeare's crown. All I claim is that for his contemporaries it served as a revelation of the troubled spirit of the most puzzling and the most canvassed character of the time. And if this be so, then something else follows: Shakespeare loved Essex, loved him more than most and admired him, this side idolatry, as much as any. Thus he not only shared in the general horror and grief at the earl's fall; he felt it in a personal fashion. The rebellion and execution, followed by the rewriting of *Hamlet* as an everlasting memorial to his friend, were—can we doubt it?—the most profound experiences he had ever passed through. For more than two years, from 1601 to 1603, he writes nothing, and when he next gives the world a play it is *All's Well that Ends Well*! What a play! What a title! It is his first bow to the new court.

VI

THE RAZOR-EDGE

I have of late—but wherefore I know not—lost all my mirth,
foregone all custom of exercises; and indeed it goes so heavily
with my disposition that this goodly frame, the earth, seems to
me a sterile promontory, this most excellent canopy, the air,
look you, this majestical roof fretted with golden fire, why, it
appears no other thing to me than a foul and pestilent con-
gregation of vapours. What a piece of work is a man! how noble
in reason; how infinite in faculty, in form, and moving; how
express and admirable in action; how like an angel in apprehension; how like a god! the beauty of the world; the paragon
of animals. And yet, to me, what is this quintessence of dust?
man delights not me; no, nor woman neither, though by your
smiling you seem to say so.

Hamlet, II. ii. 307–22.

SETTING aside the theories just elaborated, the
notion of a tragic mood as the source of Shakespeare's tragedies has still to be faced in general
terms. Many deny altogether, not only that his
moods can be known, but that, even if they could,
they would bear any relation to his dramas. Art
is one thing, life another; and whatever his personal
griefs or passions may have been, he was a professional dramatist, forced to provide comedy or
tragedy for his company according to their needs
at the moment. And critics who hold that his main
interest in his plays was the money and position he
got out of them, go on to ask how it is possible the
change from comedy to tragedy can have been due
to any tragic mood when, just as it was taking
place, he was attaining a height of success beyond
not only anything hitherto achieved by himself but

by any other poet or dramatist of his time. They
point out that when he came to write *Hamlet* he
was earning round about £400 a year, which we
must multiply by ten to give its equivalent in
modern money; that the Heralds' College had in
1596 granted his father the coat of arms originally
petitioned for in 1568, so that he was now able to
describe himself as "William Shakespeare, of Strat-
ford-upon-Avon, in the County of Warwick, gentleman"; that in 1597 this new-made gentleman had
purchased the largest and finest mansion in Stratford, New Place, respectfully known to the in-
habitants as "the Great House"; that undergraduate
plays at Cambridge between 1597 and 1600 and
allusions to him by critics like Francis Meres, who
wrote in 1598, show him as the most famous and
popular author of the age, his portrait sought for
by students to hang in their studies and himself
hailed as equal to Ovid as a poet and to Plautus
and Seneca as a writer of comedy and tragedy; and
finally that the mill was going well enough for his
company to erect an entirely new playhouse, called
the Globe, in 1599.

All this may be admitted, and more. One indication of Shakespeare's prosperity is that from 1601
onwards his output of plays falls off from his previous
rate of about three per annum to one; and it looks
as if he were now in a position to make terms with
his company which would allow him more leisure.
And part of the bargain may well have been that
he should leave comedy to others, and devote himself in the main to tragedy. After all, he had carried

comedy as far as it was possible to take it; he could hardly better *Twelfth Night*, while Falstaff had been such a roaring success that he had had to kill him off in self-protection. Tragedy, on the other hand, in spite of early efforts, was still comparatively unexplored. It beckoned him as the austere but majestic mountain top beckons the climber still treading the smiling valley-slopes. "Things unattempted yet" were always attractive to Shakespeare. Critics write as if he only experimented in his first period: he was always experimenting, always pressing forward into new country, trying out new themes, deepening and developing his grasp of character, making finer and more intricate the texture of his blank verse, originating fresh dramatic types. He could not stop growing, he hated repeating himself, and he delighted in sudden turns, his departure to Stratford in 1612 being the most striking of them all. What then more natural than that he should, after Falstaff and Feste, lay comedy aside and set himself to invent an absolutely novel kind of drama, which we now call Shakespearian tragedy?

It was not as if he would leave London without a great comic dramatist. In September 1598, the very month of the first recorded performance of *Julius Caesar*, he and his company were playing Ben Jonson's earliest comedy, *Every Man in his Humour*, the acceptance of which had been due, according to a credible tradition, to the good offices of Shakespeare himself. A year later came *Every Man out of his Humour*, also played by the Chamberlain's

Men, and though a literary and theatrical quarrel, which involved most of the dramatists of the day (including even Shakespeare as Hamlet's famous reference to the matter in Act ii, Scene ii, shows), led to an estrangement for some years, Jonson was writing for them again about 1605 and gave them his best work, *Volpone* and *The Alchemist*. Furthermore, the accession of James made it possible to revive a number of Shakespeare's comedies which were unknown to the new court, and especially to its new queen, Anne of Denmark, who was even more attached to masques and plays than her consort. Accordingly, we find *The Comedy of Errors*, *Love's Labour's Lost*, *The Merchant of Venice* (this in particular took the fancy of James I), and *The Merry Wives of Windsor* being acted at court in the winter of 1604–5. Nor was Jonson the only alternative to Shakespeare the company possessed. An obscure and very inferior dramatist called George Wilkins began to do hack work for them about this time, and his hand may be seen, I think, in more than one play in the First Folio. We may add here that later on, in 1609 or 1610, Beaumont and Fletcher also came to Shakespeare's relief with their *Philaster*, the earliest of many plays for his company by these famous collaborators.

Everything, in short, seemed to conspire to make it easy for Shakespeare both to slacken the pace of his production and to turn from comedy to tragedy. Not that there is the slightest indication—if we set aside the silence of 1601–3—of any diminution of power, either poetic or dramatic. All the accumulated experience and practised skill of the years 1590 to 1600, with a power and depth hitherto unfound, seem to be focused upon the writing of the titanic plays he now creates. Reduction in speed does not imply any flagging of energy. On the contrary, the concentration of effort required for the composition of an *Othello*, a *King Lear*, a *Macbeth*, or an *Antony and Cleopatra* may well have cost Shakespeare as much expenditure of spirit as any three histories or comedies. An almost superhuman intensity is indeed the most striking feature of all these four colossal plays. One imagines weeks, perhaps months, of more or less quiet preparation; and then one day the matter begins to take fire under the fashioning hands, burns to a white heat in which both creator and creation are fused and molten into a fluid chaos of volcanic passion, until, by an enormous effort of will, art assumes control, the dramatist subdues both himself and his material; and, after who can tell what agonising period of moulding and compression, a new world is born— the dim vast tempestuous universe of mad Lear and his three daughters, the close sultry torture-chamber with Iago gloating over his victim on the rack, the hell in which Macbeth and his Lady grope to their foul deeds, and obscene witches hover through the fog and filthy air. And once the play is finished— something like exhaustion surely follows. There are limits to human nature, and it is not to be supposed that even a Shakespeare, having just completed *King Lear*, washed his hands and cried "Fie upon this quiet life! I want work". More than one

indication—the presence (as I believe) of a colla-
borating hand in *Measure for Measure*, the failure to
finish *Timon of Athens*, and the comparative empti-
ness of *Coriolanus*, point to weariness and reaction,
a refusal of the over-driven spirit to respond to the
spur. It was assuredly no decline in dramatic capability or intellectual grasp which led to Shakespeare's
turning his back upon comedy.

He "played the sedulous ape", say some, and
was following the fashion here as elsewhere. He
tended to take hints from others in his early days,
rather than lead himself, as we have seen; and it is
certain that towards the end of the century "melancholy" became very much the vogue both in letters
and in life. This was not due to the fall of Essex,
since Shakespeare is already laughing at it in his
portrait of the melancholy Jaques. Yet there can
be no doubt that the catastrophe of 1600–1 immensely strengthened an already existing tendency.
Nor did the accession of James, bringing the release
of Southampton from prison, and the return of
many exiles, bring also with it the restoration of
merry England. The new court gave itself up to
pleasure of all kinds, and spent lavishly upon
masques and plays; so lavishly indeed that the
extravagance did something to precipitate the financial crisis of Charles's reign. James too showered
special favours upon Shakespeare and his company,
who now became "The King's Men" and the
leading players Grooms of His Majesty's Chamber.

And yet the glory had departed; a shadow lay
across the land, the shadow of the tomb; and the

air seemed thick with the breath of corruption. James made short work with the "spaciousness" of the old days: peace was concluded with Spain, and Raleigh shut up in the Tower. And what a successor he was to Elizabeth! Gloriana had been shrewish, incapable of delicacy, close-fisted, cold-hearted, and in her later years hideous and violent; but she kept her dignity to the end, and was always "mere English". James was a Scot who never understood England, or even realised he misunderstood her, while "his big head, his slobbering tongue, his quilted clothes, his ricketty legs, his goggle eyes...his gabble and rodomontade, his want of personal dignity, his vulgar buffoonery, his pedantry, his contemptible cowardice" disgusted all who had to do with him. As for the court it became a drink-shop, and in some quarters little better than a brothel; the favourite Robert Carr, in particular, introducing a strain into public life which reminds us of the poison and debauchery of the decadent Italian renaissance. Such things did nothing to stem the tide of melancholy, which deepened and became more extravagant as time went on (despite ebbings and cross-currents like the later romances of Shakespeare and the work of Beaumont and Fletcher), until it came to rage with frenzied madness in the plays of Webster, Ford and Tourneur, and to sweep with sombre magnificence through the sermons of Dean Donne.

Nevertheless, when all is said, I believe that Shakespeare's tragedies reflect personal feeling and inner spiritual experience. Some artists have been able to keep their lives and their creations in different compartments. Others, and I think most of the greatest, decidedly have not. Dante and Milton did not scruple to give utterance to their loves and hates in epic. The Olympian Goethe is autobiographical from first to last. And how wonderfully the lives of such differing geniuses as Wordsworth, Beethoven and Dostoieffsky illuminate their works! Keats certainly did not subscribe to the doctrine of the impersonality of the poet. "A man's life of any worth is a continual allegory," he writes; and again "Shakespeare led a life of allegory: his works are the comments on it". To adopt the opposite view is only possible if the tragedies be taken as individual and detached products of genius; look at Shakespeare's dramatic work from 1601 to 1608 as a whole, and the conclusion is, I think, irresistible that, for whatever cause, Shakespeare was subject at this time to a dominant mood of gloom and dejection, which on one occasion at least brought him to the verge of madness. No doubt he marched with the spirit of his age; but that does not imply insincerity. On the contrary, he was himself at once the very core of that spirit and its chief exponent. Further, his expression of it strengthened its hold both upon his contemporaries and himself, until in the end the mood passed from him.

One indication that this mood was

Felt in the blood and felt along the heart,

and not just an artistic pose, is the nature of the comedies belonging to this period. When his com-

pany asked him for a comedy in 1600 he gave them
Twelfth Night; in 1603 he could do nothing for
them but *All's Well*, and followed it up next year
with the equally acrid *Measure for Measure*, while
though *Troilus and Cressida* was probably written for
private performance in the autumn of 1600, it to some
extent anticipates the other two. The note of them
all is disillusionment and cynicism, the air is cheer-
less and often unwholesome, the wit mirthless, the
bad characters contemptible or detestable, the good
ones unattractive. Helena in *All's Well* is a most
admirable and noble lady; yet everything she does
sets our teeth on edge. The sainted Isabella, wrapt
in her selfish chastity, is no better; our hearts warm
more to the wretched boy who in terror of death
is ready to sacrifice his sister's honour. Sir Edmund
Chambers even detects in the "old fantastical duke
of dark corners", who plays the part of providence
with such strange whimsicality and incompetence,
"a satirical intention of Shakespeare towards theories
about the moral government of the universe which,
for the time being at least, he does not share".

Measure for Measure is a comedy only in the technical sense that it concludes with the chief characters
still alive; its sombre prison scenes, its grotesque
and hideous figures of Abhorson, the executioner,
and Barnardine, the condemned desperado, its
magnificent speeches in contempt of life and in
terror of death, its sinister hypocrite Angelo, and its
riff-raff of bawds, beadles and fribbles, all stamp
it as from the tragic mint, all show us a very different
Shakespeare from the calm, impersonal philosopher

generally believed in. And neither *All's Well* nor
Measure for Measure, I am convinced, is wholly
Shakespeare's; even for this kind of comedy he had
no inclination, and left a torso for Wilkins or some
other hack to provide with arms and legs.

And yet these plays, above all others by Shakespeare, should be easiest for our own day to understand. *Measure for Measure* is written in much
the same key as *Point Counter Point* and others of
Mr Aldous Huxley's novels. The hatred of sentimentalism and romance, the savage determination
to tear aside all veils, to expose reality in its
crudity and hideousness, the self-laceration, weariness, discord, cynicism and disgust of our modern
"literature of negation" all belonged to Shakespeare about 1603; and he would well have understood Mr T. S. Eliot's *The Waste Land*, with lines
like these :

> What are the roots that clutch, what branches grow
> Out of this stony rubbish? Son of man,
> You cannot say, or guess, for you know only
> A heap of broken images, where the sun beats,
> And the dead tree gives no shelter, the cricket no relief,
> And the dry stone no sound of water. Only
> There is a shadow under this red rock,
> (Come in under the shadow of this red rock),
> And I will show you something different from either
> Your shadow at morning striding behind you
> Or your shadow at evening rising to meet you;
> I will show you fear in a handful of dust.

And his mood sprang from circumstances very
much like ours. The fundamental cause of our
despair is, of course, the Great War, which began
in a temper of exaltation, best expressed in the

poetry of Rupert Brooke, ended in a holocaust of blood and mud, and was followed—our war to end war—by the cynical Peace of Versailles. The Elizabethan catastrophe described the same curve within a narrower ambit: national elation after the defeat of the Armada, best expressed in *Henry V*, the crash of Essex, and the squalid peace of James.

Another personal clue, also with a close parallel in the literature of to-day, is the strain of sex-nausea which runs through almost everything he wrote after 1600. "Sweet Desire" has turned sour! It has become ferocious also; Venus and the boar have changed roles; and Shakespeare was to have no security until the beast is fast chained to the rock beneath Prospero's cell. Whatever the cause, whether it had something to do, as many think, with the dark-eyed mistress of the *Sonnets*, though that episode must have been long past in 1601, or simply to the general morbidity of the age, certain it is the change is there. And that it was not a mere trick found useful to a practising dramatist is, I think, proved by its presence in the ravings of Lear, where there is no dramatic reason for it at all. Further, it is difficult to avoid associating it with personal jealousy of some kind. Jealousy is the mainspring of no less than four plays: *Troilus and Cressida, Othello, Winter's Tale,* and *Cymbeline,* while there are traces of it in *Antony and Cleopatra,* and one may suspect that it furnished material for the scene between Hamlet and his mother. That "couch for luxury and damned incest", which, unseen, is ever present to the mind both of Hamlet and of the

audience, is, I think, symbolic. Far more than the
murder, it is this which transforms the Prince's
imagination into something "as foul as Vulcan's
stithy". The imagination of Othello is as foul, and
more explicit. Even Lear, as I have just said,
broods "over the nasty sty" and begs "an ounce
of civet to sweeten his imagination", while to
Posthumus and Leontes is given utterance scarcely
less outspoken than Othello's. Above all in *Timon
of Athens*, which breathes a hatred of mankind that
rivals Swift's, nearly a whole act is devoted to the
unsavoury topic. Collect these passages together,
face them as they should be faced, and the conclusion is inescapable that the defiled imagination
of which Shakespeare writes so often, and depicts
in metaphor so nakedly material, must be his own.

Young Love, which had once been the meaning of
the universe, a triumphant deity, upon whose altar,
decked out in all the pomp and splendour of poetry,
boy Romeo and girl Juliet delight to die upon a kiss,
goes out a bedraggled cupid with the sad youth
Troilus, and does not re-enter Shakespeare's world
until Florizel, led by his falcon, discovers Perdita.
Its place, however, is not left vacant; Lust has it.

The bitter comedies are intensely interesting as
illustrations of Shakespeare's mood, but they are a
side-show. From 1601 to 1608 he is absorbed in
tragedy, and the path he treads during these eight
years may be likened to a mountain track which,
rising gently from the plain, grows ever narrower,
until at the climax of the ascent it dwindles to the
thinnest razor-edge, a glacial arête, with the abyss

on either hand, and then once again grows secure for foothold as it broadens out and gradually descends into the valley beyond.

Eight plays compose this tragic course. The first, *Julius Caesar*, written a little before the tragic period proper, is a tragedy of weakness not of evil. In *Hamlet* the forces of evil are active and sinister, though still the prevailing note is weakness of character. *Othello* gives us, if we put aside Richard Crookback as a crude juvenile effort, Shakespeare's earliest creation of a character wholly evil, and at the same time Iago's victim is blameless—human weakness is no longer allowed to share the responsibility with heaven. *King Lear* carries us right to the edge of the abyss, for here horror is piled upon horror and pity on pity, to make the greatest monument of human misery and despair in the literature of the world; and one purpose of this tremendous catastrophic play was undoubtedly to bring home to those who watched it the terror of Life and the unspeakable depths of man's brutality. To hold a mirror up to nature! But if nature was this gorgon crowned with writhing serpents, might not the artist holding the mirror himself be turned to stone? Shakespeare came very near to madness in *Lear*. How near may be seen in *Timon of Athens*, which Sir Edmund Chambers, while striving to prove himself the most objective and cautious of modern critics, has suggested must have been written "under conditions of mental and perhaps physical stress, which led to a breakdown". Yet he pushed forward, for in *Macbeth*, the next play, we feel somehow, terrible as the atmosphere still is, that Shakespeare is himself not so deeply involved, while once again human beings, Macbeth and his wife, take their share of responsibility with the cosmic forces of evil for the crimes and disasters that occur. And in *Antony and Cleopatra*, one of the very greatest of Shakespeare's plays, about which, however, we can say nothing in a book of this scope, the tension is altogether slacker: indeed, we return in the last act to something of the exaltation which *Romeo and Juliet* inspires. As for *Coriolanus*, its fault is that the dramatist seems hardly to be concerned in it at all; his spirit is elsewhere upon some new quest.

How did Shakespeare save his soul alive in this, one of the most perilous and arduous adventures ever undertaken by the spirit of man? With a very different view of life from that of Dostoieffsky, he nevertheless won through in much the same fashion as the great Russian hacked out a path from *The House of the Dead* to *The Brothers Karamazov*. As the forces of evil close in upon him, as the possibilities of human bestiality are more and more revealed, there are revealed at the same time other possibilities, possibilities of nobility, of spiritual grandeur, of magnificent and indomitable will, of sheer exuberant vitality as great in its way as Falstaff's. It is the spectacle of the majestic peaks that surround him, Mount Othello, Mount Lear, and the twin heights of Macbeth and his Lady, of Antony and his mistress, which keep him from slipping into the abyss of madness, brutality and despair that yawns beneath his tottering feet. They are part of his vision of the universe, yet not wholly of his invention. They come upon him inevitably, almost unexpectedly, as he gropes his way blindly forward. Indeed they and the abyss are one; both are features of the same tremendous and appalling panorama which comprises the heights and depths of human nature. There is nothing mysterious about this, or at least nothing peculiar to Shakespeare. He could no more have evaded Lear than Dostoieffsky could have evaded Myshkin or Emily Brontë Heathcliff. Nor is it a case of contrast, of setting white against black, of opposing virtue to vice; for, as often as not, these giants possess as much terror as beauty, and we cannot attach our little moral labels to the everlasting hills. Neither did Shakespeare set out to "justify the ways of God to man", to show virtue triumphant, or to prove anything at all. He started from nothing, for when he wrote the bitter comedies he quite obviously believed in nothing; he was as cynical as Iago, and as disillusioned as Macbeth, though he still retained, unlike the first, his sensitiveness and, unlike the second, his hatred of cruelty, hypocrisy and ingratitude.

The tragedies, therefore, were an experiment, the result of which he could not guess beforehand, and the purpose of which was to mirror the whole meaning of Life, if indeed there was any meaning at all to mirror. And he began as savagely as the Elizabethan hangman with his knife. In a notable essay on *Measure for Measure*, Sir Edmund Chambers points to "the remorseless analysis which probes the inmost being of man and strips him naked before the spectators while he—

> Plays such fantastic tricks before high heaven,
> As make the angels weep.

It is the temper of the inquisitor; and you can but shudder as a soul is brought into the torture-chamber and shrivels to nothingness before some sharp test of circumstance". The inquisitor is present in all the tragedies. So ruthless is he, so uncompromising, that it is easy to see where Iago comes from. The human devil who delights in contemplating the writhings of a tortured spirit is a part of Shakespeare himself, the projection into the moral sphere of an overmastering dramatic impulse. Yet there are critics who declare that Shakespeare never judges! To say so is to rob him of an eye. Further, this pitilessness is our security. It assures us that he will spare neither himself nor us; that he will blink no facts, stoop to no subterfuge, offer no false hopes or mystical dream-ladder of escape. Nothing but the truth, the whole appalling truth, will satisfy him. The experiment must go forward, even if it brings himself and his entire universe to annihilation.

Yet Shakespeare the inquisitor is only part of the story. Strangely and wonderfully, there is Shakespeare the lover to be reckoned with too. He cannot put that from him, however much he agonises or loathes. This then is the secret of his escape from disaster on the heights. He kept his balance, the tragic balance between truth and beauty, between inexorable judgment and divine compassion. And this balance was at once a supreme spiritual achievement and a triumph of dramatic technique, since it was a development and a consummation of all the accumulated skill and knowledge of the ten previous years. In 1599 he little knew what awaited him; yet when the storm burst he displayed what Bridges has called "masterful administration of the unforeseen". Finally, his victory was a victory for the whole human race. *King Lear* is a piece of exploration, more dearly won and far more significant than that of a Shackleton or an Einstein; for, while they have enlarged the bounds of human knowledge, *Lear* has revealed the human spirit as of greater sublimity than we could otherwise have dreamed.

The tragic balance may, of course, be seen in all the great tragedies, is indeed the clue to their true interpretation. I must, however, be content here to illustrate its relevance by a closer study of the greatest, the play just mentioned. I have already pointed out that as Shakespeare's tragic imagination deepened, it came to dwell less and less upon faults of character and more and more upon the forces of evil in the universe. *King Lear* combines the method of *Hamlet* with that of *Othello*; that is to say, it is at once a drama of character and a drama of destiny. Lear is a king "more sinned against than sinning". Hell, in the person of his two daughters and in the symbol of the storm, seems to rise up in full panoply, first to crush the old man's pride, then to overthrow his intellect, and last of all to break his heart. And yet Lear *has* sinned, so that the play is not a picture only of goodness over-whelmed by evil but also, as we noticed in speaking of *Richard II*, of an irascible old tyrant, spoilt by a long life of uncontrolled and immoderate use of power, rising through the discipline of humiliation and disaster to a height unequalled elsewhere in Shakespeare. Gloucester's cry

> As flies to wanton boys, are we to the gods,
> They kill us for their sport—

is for many, perhaps for most, the moral of the play, and there is much to support it. Lear invokes the heavens against filial ingratitude, but instead of hearing his appeal for justice they join "with two pernicious daughters" their "high engendered battles" of storm and rain, thunder and lightning, to chastise him. At every turn destiny, or God, pursues him as with hatred until, when we hear of Cordelia's army being crushed and herself taken prisoner with her father, we feel, as in the book of Job or in a novel by Thomas Hardy, that we human beings are puppets,

> But helpless pieces of the game He plays
> Upon this chequer-board of nights and days;
> Hither and thither moves, and checks and slays,
> And one by one back in the closet lays.

And then the heavens open to discharge their last dreadful bolt, and for some of us at least the mood changes. When Lear enters, in that final and most terrible scene, with Cordelia dead in his arms, we cannot think of him any longer as a fly or a puppet or a chessman. What the meaning of

Life may be we know no more than before, but we marvel at the greatness of man and at what man can endure. Lear is like some peak of anguish, an eternal and sublime symbol of the majesty of humanity, of the victory of spirit over the worst that fate can do against it. This last scene reminds us, inevitably, of Calvary. But it is a human Calvary; there is no resurrection to follow, not a hint of a Father in heaven. And yet the universe in which Lear is possible cannot be wholly evil, since he is part of it, and Cordelia is part of it, and the possibility of such souls may even be a clue to its meaning.

And there is something more. The Lear that dies is not a Lear defiant, but a Lear redeemed. His education is complete, his regeneration accomplished. The headstrong, ungovernable, tempestuous old despot, after passing through the purgatory of insanity and the brief heaven of reconciliation with his Cordelia, has become "a very foolish, fond old man", with no claim except for forgiveness and no desire except for love. This is not the last stage of imbecility and dotage, but recovery. Never is Lear greater, more tremendous, more his real self, than in the final moment, when he confronts "high-judging Jove" not with

> the unconquerable will,
> And study of revenge, immortal hate,
> And courage never to submit or yield,

but with the oblation of a broken heart. And as we turn our eyes from a scene too terrible and pitiable to be endured, is it our weakness or a hint

of the Truth that brings back to us words uttered
by Lear himself on the way to prison just before:

> Upon such sacrifices, my Cordelia,
> The gods themselves throw incense?

Men will discuss the meaning of *King Lear* to the
end of time, as they will discuss the meaning of the
universe, for the two meanings are the same. The
one certain message of the play is that nothing is
certain. Shakespeare has no solution to offer, but
he gives us something far greater. He has fashioned
a mirror of art in which, more successfully than any
man before or since, he has caught the whole of
Life and focused it to one intense and burning
point of terror and beauty. And in so doing he
found salvation. For, though the ravings of *Timon
of Athens* show how near he came to plunging head-
long into the abyss, *Macbeth*, which is almost a
morality play, and the marvellous *Antony and
Cleopatra*, in which love lifts a libertine and a harlot
into the sublime atmosphere of Romeo and Juliet,
prove that he kept his balance and passed on.

VII

THE ENCHANTED ISLAND

Congreeing in a full and natural close,
Like music.

Henry V, i. ii. 182-3.

Aʙᴏᴜᴛ 1608 or 1609 a change comes over the
art and temper of Shakespeare, as profound though
less sudden than that which took place in 1601.
We pass from tragedy to romance, that is to say
from plays that end in disaster to those the final
act of which is given up to happy reconciliations
and forgiveness, and from a mood which looks like
pessimism to one that has been described, a little
rashly, as "a boundless and confident optimism".
With the new themes and the new mood has come
too, as ever with Shakespeare, a new poetic style
and a new dramatic structure.

The school that regards Shakespeare as the
great dramatic time-server of the Elizabethan and
Jacobean age accounts for all this, in its usual
manner, as part of a general shift of literary taste.
They quote Middleton and Dekker who in 1610
are declaring that

Tragic passion
And such grave stuff is this day out of fashion.

They remind us that Beaumont and Fletcher, who
attain their first great success with *Philaster*, produced between 1608 and 1610, are writing very
similar plays to those of Shakespeare's final period,
and they even detect deliberate imitation of the

play just mentioned in *Cymbeline*. They see in the masque-like quality of these plays the influence of the masques at court. And they point out that the years 1608–12, during which Shakespeare was composing them, were exactly those when the attractive and universally beloved Prince Henry (who was created Prince of Wales in 1610 and died in 1612 at the age of eighteen) would have been a power in London and displaying a keen interest in the theatre, while some have even gone so far as to discover in Florizel and Ferdinand tributes to his youth and charm. To which other critics retort that there is no reason whatever for supposing that Shakespeare did not start the fashion himself, that *Philaster*, the exact date of which is uncertain, is more likely to have been modelled upon *Cymbeline* than the reverse, and that, while the royal Florizel may have inspired Shakespeare to some extent, he had a Perdita of his own at Stratford in his younger daughter Judith, a girl of just over twenty, living in surroundings far more resembling those of the fourth act of *The Winter's Tale* than anything which could be found about the court.

Sir Edmund Chambers who takes this line attributes the change in the first place to illness. He finds *King Lear* a wholly pessimistic play, an "indictment of the forces that make sport of man's nothingness", and he sees in the terrible and unfinished *Timon* evidence of a complete breakdown. In a word, Shakespeare plunges for a time into the abyss. Prostration follows, but the quiet of Stratford and the care of good Dr Hall, who marries his daughter Susanna in 1607, the very year when the illness, if it happened at all, is likely to have taken place, gradually restores him to health. It is, however, a different Shakespeare who rises from the sick-bed. "The transition from the tragedies to the romances is not an evolution but a revolution. There has been some mental process such as the psychology of religion would call a conversion. Obviously the philosophy of the tragedies is not a Christian philosophy, and in a sense that of the romances is." And the theory is then rounded off with a reference to the legend, which goes back to Richard Davies a Gloucestershire clergyman at the end of the seventeenth century, that Shakespeare "dyed a papist".

There is something in all this. *Timon* may well be connected with a serious illness, which may in turn equally well be due to the terrible strain which the writing of the tragedies placed upon the dramatist. Yet the view is altogether too highly coloured and melodramatic, far more so than the facts require. It is wrong, too, to regard Shakespeare as a "philosopher" trying to solve the problems of the universe; it is wrong to assume that *Lear* is anti-Christian in tone or that *The Tempest* is the reverse. As for "dying a papist", that is just the sort of story a parson of the time would delight in crediting, and circulating, about "one of those harlotry players" who, by amassing wealth acquired in infamy, had taken upon him to become a great person. I do not believe it; and there are no signs whatever of "papistry" in *The Tempest*. That Shakespeare underwent at this time something like a "conversion" is probable; but it was certainly not a doctrinal one, hardly a religious one in the ordinary sense of the word. Above all Sir Edmund is committed by his theory to a "sudden" and "complete reversal of standards and values", and he is therefore obliged to separate the writing of *Timon* from that of *Lear*, and to suppose that it followed *Antony and Cleopatra* and *Coriolanus*, which, if the tone of these plays reflect anything at all of their author's state of mind, is surely absurd. The date of *Timon* is unknown, but unless it be the still-born twin of *Lear* then we may give up talking about Shakespearian moods altogether; while the two Roman plays clearly mark a relaxation of strain.

I shall return to the literary implications of this theory in a moment. But first another biographical point must be dealt with. Many writers assume that Shakespeare was more or less of a convalescent in his last years, that his grip was loosening and his brain softening. I can see no evidence whatever for this in the plays themselves. Turning to invent a new form of drama to match a new mood, Shakespeare as usual experiments before he achieves exactly what he aims at, and by the side of *The Tempest* its immediate predecessors, it is true, seem loose-knit. Yet they are lovely things in themselves —*Cymbeline*, it must be remembered, was Tennyson's favourite play, and his precious copy was buried with him; while *The Tempest*, as a piece of sheer artistry, is surely the most consummate of all Shakespeare's masterpieces. But why did not Shakespeare write anything after *The Tempest*? Is there not something odd, enquires the Shylock school of criticism, in a man giving up a lucrative profession at the age of forty-eight, leaving London at the height of his fame, and retiring to an obscure provincial town like Stratford? And there follows talk of Bright's disease, or even worse things are whispered.

The problem of the retirement is, as I shall later show, closely related to that of the "conversion". But two things may be said at once about it. In the first place, the break with London in 1612 was clearly deliberate, and a decision taken when Shakespeare was apparently in perfect health. *The Tempest* proves this; for *The Tempest*, as most readers have agreed, is on the face of it Shakespeare's farewell to the theatre, and *The Tempest* was not written by a sick man. And in the second place, there is not a hint either in contemporary record or local tradition that Shakespeare suffered disability or disease of any sort during his later years. On the contrary, all we can glean points to cheerfulness and happiness. His first biographer Rowe, writing in 1709, declares that "the latter part of his life was spent, as all men of good sense will wish theirs may be, in ease, retirement, and the conversation of friends", while he also asserts that Shakespeare was well acquainted with many gentlemen of the neighbourhood. There were visitors too from London. We are told of a convivial meeting with Drayton and Ben Jonson shortly before the end, which does not suggest failing health and certainly suggests high spirits. The information comes from John Ward, vicar of Stratford from 1662 to 1681, who adds "it seems" that they "drank too hard, for Shakespeare died of a fever there contracted". The supposition of the parson we may discount, like the tale of dying a papist. But we have no reason to disbelieve his statement about the "fever"; many in Stratford as early as 1662 would remember what the great man died of, and Ward who was interested in medicine would take careful note of such a fact. Shakespeare, we may therefore assume, was carried off by some epidemic four years after he had turned his back upon London.

To understand Shakespeare's retirement, we must return to 1608, try and fathom his "conversion", and study his last plays. For here as in everything else about him the poet was father to the man, and Keats is the truest guide when he tells us that "Shakespeare led a life of allegory; his works are the comments upon it".

As I have said, sickness of body as well as sickness of spirit there may well have been after the completion of *Lear*, but illness is not necessary to explain the lifting of the clouds in *Antony and Cleopatra*, the ebb of the tragic tide visible in *Coriolanus*, the dawn of a new mood in *Pericles* and *Cymbeline*. And the "conversion" itself is of course a poetic one—none the less real or profound for that! Accordingly we must go for helpful analogies, not to the theological or moral sphere, but to the realm of art.

Beethoven's last phase possesses points of similarity which it would be fascinating to explore, had I the musical knowledge or insight. Let me instead briefly consider three literary parallels. First there is *The Book of Job*, that marvellous poem on the meaning of the universe, a theme which it handles artistically and not philosophically, exactly as Shakespeare handles it in *Lear*. But *Job* embraces more than *Lear*; it includes the recovery as well as the anguish. And what is it that brings the recovery about? Certainly not the philosophers; there are three of them, each with his special solution, and they are called "Job's comforters" because they bring no comfort. The healing comes, neither from argument nor statement, but from a contemplation of the beauty of the world, the morning stars singing together, the majesty of the sea, the strength and loveliness of the animals, the glory of the creation of God. Or take Dostoieffsky, whose cosmic novels are the nearest approach to Shakespeare's tragedies in modern literature. He too in the terrible *Crime and Punishment*, *The Idiot*, and *The Possessed* treads the razor-edge and only comes through as by a miracle. In the last and greatest of his books, which has points of affinity with *The Tempest*, the miracle is in part explained, and we see that salvation has been won through a return to the grand simplicities of life, typified by the divine Alyosha and his boys, and by the story of the marriage at Cana of Galilee.

But Shakespeare was English, and the closest analogy to his conversion is that of another English poet, a poet who experienced it at the beginning not near the end of his career, who had nevertheless, like Shakespeare, passed through a spiritual crisis, leading him to the gates of madness, who had dreamed of an age of reason,

> France standing on the top of golden hours,
> And human nature seeming born again,

had seen the vision dissolve in blood and terror; and had come to realise that the attempt to overthrow the social structure meant striking at the very roots of the spirit of man. Gradually, by the help of a woman, his sister (as Shakespeare perhaps by his daughter), the spiritual convalescent recovered his lost self and his first love, his love of the countryside on which his infant eyes had rested, amid which he had grown to manhood, from which he had learned to become a poet. The revulsion of feeling was complete. He seemed to have escaped from subjection to some barren witch who had offered him an impossible and detestable mirage in exchange for the paradise that lay around him. Nature, the birds, youth, the peasant, the simple traffic of family life, all that drew blood from that accumulated wisdom of centuries which we call instinct and tradition, were the only teachers, the only healers.

I use words I wrote about Wordsworth five years ago, without a thought of Shakespeare in my mind. The parallel is not exact, of course; history does not repeat herself. But the crisis and its occasion, the conversion and its cause, are extraordinarily similar.

Wordsworth recovered by falling in love a second time with the Lake country; Shakespeare by falling in love a second time with Stratford. But let Wordsworth himself speak for the creator of *Lear*.

> These beauteous forms,
> Through a long absence, have not been to me
> As is a landscape to a blind man's eye:
> But oft, in lonely rooms, and 'mid the din
> Of towns and cities, I have owed to them,
> In hours of weariness, sensations sweet,
> Felt in the blood, and felt along the heart;
> And passing even into my purer mind,
> With tranquil restoration....Nor less, I trust,
> To them I may have owed another gift,
> Of aspect more sublime; that blessed mood,
> In which the burthen of the mystery,
> In which the heavy and the weary weight
> Of all this unintelligible world,
> Is lightened:—that serene and blessed mood,
> In which the affections gently lead us on,—
> Until, the breath of this corporeal frame
> And even the motion of our human blood
> Almost suspended, we are laid asleep
> In body, and become a living soul:
> While with an eye made quiet by the power
> Of harmony, and the deep power of joy,
> We see into the life of things.

There is no more wonderful description of poetic ecstasy in all poetry than this, and there is no better illustration of its truth than *The Tempest*. Wordsworth explains the last plays of Shakespeare, and the last plays lend to Wordsworth's lines the force of a new revelation.

Shakespeare fell in love with Stratford, with its memories, its quiet pastures and wide skies, with all the wild life of bird and beast and flower, with the pleasant friendships and domesticities of the little town, with his house and garden, with his own family, and especially perhaps with his younger daughter. Can any explanation of his retirement be more natural and more complete than this, if we remember that when poets love they love with a passion which cannot be gainsaid? One can feel it growing in the plays, from the contrast drawn by Bellarius between the slippery life of the court and the honest freedom of the countryside, through the sheep-shearing scene of *The Winter's Tale*, up to the inaccessible island cut off from civilisation, full of

Sounds and sweet airs that give delight and hurt not.

But most of all is it felt in the innocent figures, especially of young girls, that now take the centre of his stage: Marina, playing with her flowers by the water's brink, Imogen and the "flower-like boys, Guiderius and Arviragus", Perdita as Flora at the country-feast with her Florizel, and to crown all, the peerless couple Miranda and Ferdinand.

It meant of course giving up his art, for though *The Tempest* at any rate was I think mostly written at Stratford, that was not Shakespeare's way and in the nature of things could not last. So a choice had to be made, and *The Tempest* tells us what it cost him.

And yet, he had surely given the world enough! Twenty years' slavery at his desk, and the handling of thirty-six plays; what more did they want?

If he stayed on in London, could he ever write better love-plays than *Romeo and Juliet* and *Antony and Cleopatra*, or better comedies than *As You Like It* and *Twelfth Night*, or better tragedies than *Othello*, *Lear* and *Macbeth*, or better fairy-plays than *A Midsummer-Night's Dream* and *The Tempest*; or create greater characters than Shylock, Falstaff, Hamlet, Lady Macbeth and Cleopatra? His company could get on without him; dramatists had become plentiful, and this Beaumont and Fletcher pair had the trick to entertain the court people well enough. Not that there was any fear of his own plays going out of fashion; as long as there were King's Men in England and a King to perform for, they would be in demand—he knew their worth. Some folk would have him print them; but printing was bad business for a playhouse, and the printing-press was a new-fangled toy which had never taken his fancy. Neighbour Field had made a fair job of those poems of his which had pleased his patron; what he had seen of printed plays, however, had not pleased him, least of all the plays of his own which actors had stolen or the company had sold to publishers in hard times. Besides plays were not books at all; that was one of Ben Jonson's mistakes. Ben talked of publishing "his works", but he was a bookman, even a little of a pedant, and never could understand that plays were like music which only came alive when performed. And though retirement to Stratford meant giving up the stage, one could always write poetry. *Venus and Adonis*, *Lucrece*, and the sonnets were juvenile stuff; he had had no time since to attempt anything more in that sort. But if the fit came upon him, it had to take its course, and at Stratford....First of all, however, he must order his house and garden; and he needed rest, intermission from writing, for a space of years at least.

Four years were granted. Who knows what ten or a dozen might have brought forth for English literature, or even whether his puritan son-in-law Dr Hall may not have quietly suppressed "pagan verses" found in his study of books after his death?

And so the last plays are the last we have of him. Taken in order they show "the burthen of the mystery"

> the heavy and the weary weight
> Of all this unintelligible world

growing ever lighter as

> that serene and blessed mood,
> In which the affections gently led him on

became more and more habitual. But, being the most honest poet who ever breathed, he was not going to seek an easy though false security by escape. He clung to the old mood, almost in desperation; there are more fearful scenes in *Pericles*, despite its happy ending, than in *Antony and Cleopatra*. At the outset his method is simply one of contrast, white against black, Marina the dove of innocence in the brothel, or the radiant and spotless Imogen disrobing herself while foul Iachimo lurks in his trunk. But the atmosphere of a drama depends upon its total effect, and especially the effect left by the concluding scenes.

Put to the test of theatrical performance, all four plays appear as plays of reconciliation and forgiveness. Shakespeare had always grown tender, right from the beginning, at the thought of pity, mercy, forgiveness; and his worship of them had shown itself sublime in the scenes between Lear and Cordelia. It is therefore natural enough that they should assume special prominence in the romances. Yet one cannot help wondering whether their presence in these plays was not somehow connected with the return to Stratford. Was there some feud to compose, some wrong to make amends for, before the owner of New Place could say "The air breathes upon us here most sweetly"?

In *The Winter's Tale* the two worlds are treated in a fresh and more satisfactory fashion. We begin with a little jealousy play complete in itself, Leontes being an ignoble Othello; the second part is entirely given up to the brave new world of love and beauty and innocence; and then the two are brought together cunningly in the reconciliation scene of the living statue. *The Winter's Tale* is one of the tenderest and loveliest of all Shakespeare's dramas, but it did not content him. Two separate worlds, the blessed world and the bitter world, even when reconciled in a finale do not make either one world or one play. For the problem was both a technical and a spiritual one, as is generally the case with Shakespeare, and indeed with all poets who attempt to span the whole of life. It was a problem, let me insist again, of art, not of morals or philosophy or theology. If he could once attain a vision of the two worlds and his two moods as a single harmonious whole, and could express that vision in a play as perfect in its way as *King Lear*, his spirit would be at rest and he would have earned his Stratford.

And one day the vision came, came as things often did with him from some chance event of the hour. Late in 1610 news reached London of a wreck off the Bermudas in which an English ship had gone aground and those on board had, miraculously as it seemed, come to shore upon an island very fertile but reported by all as enchanted. The news and the excitement it caused gave him his topic, and the topic solved his problem. The play should begin daringly with a wreck and a tempest, so realistic and overwhelming in its effect, that the audience would be ready to suspend all disbelief in the marvels that followed. For on the enchanted island he would bring the wrongers and the wronged together, and the two worlds should be harmonised at one spot and at one point of time. Harmonised, not opposed as on a battle-field—he would so work it that the injurers should "lie all at the mercy" of the injured, and should then be overcome, not through punishment or revenge, but by means of forgiveness and reconciliation, a reconciliation which should be sealed by love, by the blessed union of innocents from both worlds, too young to have inherited the wrongs or the guilt of either.

So far, except for the technical advance of the unity of space, time and atmosphere, the theme was much the same as that of *Pericles*, *Cymbeline*, and *The Winter's*

Tale. Yet *The Tempest* altogether transcends the aim and scope of its predecessors, and it does so largely because of this unity, or rather through the island, which is the means whereby unity both dramatic and spiritual is secured. For, what is the enchanted island but Life itself, which seems so "desert and uninhabitable" to the cynics and so green with "lush and lusty" grass to the single-minded? It is Life also as Shakespeare himself sees it with his recovered vision; once the domain of a foul witch, but now beneath the sway of a magician who controls it entirely, who keeps the evil spirits in subjection and employs the good spirits to serve his ends, and so has banished fear from it.

> Be not afeard—the isle is full of noises,
> Sounds and sweet airs that give delight and hurt not:
> Sometimes a thousand twangling instruments
> Will hum about mine ears; and sometimes voices,
> That, if I then had waked after long sleep,
> Will make me sleep again—and then in dreaming,
> The clouds methought would open, and show riches
> Ready to drop upon me, that when I waked
> I cried to dream again.

How like that is to Wordsworth in feeling, how unlike in expression!

What then is Prospero who works these marvels? He reminds us of Lear, a wronged old man, but a happier Lear with his Cordelia to share his banishment. There is, too, much of Shakespeare himself in him, as has often been observed; and I have no doubt that the dismissal of Ariel and the lines:

> I'll break my staff,
> Bury it certain fathoms in the earth,
> And deeper than did ever plummet sound
> I'll drown my book—

are his hinted farewell to the theatre, while the speech which precedes these lines is surely intended to depict the tragic mood he has just escaped. Prospero, again, has learnt that Desire may prove a savage beast, and has chained it up in a rock beneath his cell. Yet he is more than Shakespeare, he is Dramatic Poetry; just as the island is more than Life, it is Life seen in the mirror of ripe dramatic art, Life seen

> not as in the hour
> Of thoughtless youth; but hearing oftentimes
> The still sad music of humanity,
> Not harsh nor grating, though of ample power
> To chasten and subdue.

Prospero is a magician; but all that he performs is wrought by means of Ariel, who is poetic imagination. Even the turning-point of the play, his conversion from the thought of revenge to thoughts of pity and forgiveness, is prompted not by moral or religious considerations, but by Ariel. Thus Shakespeare anticipates Shelley's famous doctrine: "The great instrument of moral good is the imagination; and poetry administers to the effect by acting upon the cause". And the apocalyptic vision of the universe to which he gives utterance at the end of his masque, what is it but an interpretation of Life as a sublime dramatic poem?

> Be cheerful, sir.
> Our revels now are ended: these our actors,
> As I foretold you, were all spirits, and
> Are melted into air, into thin air,
> And like the baseless fabric of this vision,
> The cloud-capped towers, the gorgeous palaces,
> The solemn temples, the great globe itself,
> Yea, all which it inherit, shall dissolve,
> And like this insubstantial pageant faded,
> Leave not a rack behind: we are such stuff
> As dreams are made on; and our little life
> Is rounded with a sleep.

Is *The Tempest* a Christian play? It is surely a profoundly religious poem, and of a Christ-like spirit in its infinite tenderness, its all-embracing sense of pity, its conclusion of joyful atonement and forgiveness, so general that even Caliban begins to talk of "grace". But it is not in the least Christian from the theological standpoint; there is no word of God, not a hint of immortality. On the contrary, rewrite the passage just quoted in scientific prose, and we find ourselves confronted with an icy universe, utterly regardless of man and destined to ultimate extinction, which reminds us of the philosophy of Bertrand Russell. But it is not science either, and instead of depressing it elevates the spirit with the grandeur of the spectacle it presents and the magnificence of the rhetoric in which it is clothed. Questions of fact and of opinion are irrelevant here. We are in a realm beyond reason or belief; we are sharing in the beatific vision of the greatest of all dramatic poets,

> While with an eye made quiet by the power
> Of harmony, and the deep power of joy,
> We see into the life of things.

The Tempest is not then the subject of argument or explanation; it is to be accepted and experienced. Even my attempt to catch glimpses of a personal view behind its divine ecstasy (in order to rebut a powerful critic who regards the drama as a kind of hothouse, with an atmosphere compounded of disgust, boredom and phantasmagoria) misleads and offends; for, use it how we will,

> Our meddling intellect
> Misshapes the beauteous forms of things.

If we are to talk about *The Tempest*, it must be as poetry; or to compare it with anything else, it must be with other dramatic poems. It is, for instance, at once the completion and the obverse of *King Lear*. In *King Lear* Shakespeare succeeded in showing Truth, at its bleakest and most terrifying, as Beauty; in *The Tempest* he succeeded in showing Beauty, at its serenest, most magical and most blessed, as Truth. And if we are to seek his faith, we must go not to the creeds but to the poets. Keats is his nearest of kin, and the confession of Keats might have been his also:

> "Beauty is truth, truth beauty,"—that is all
> Ye know on earth, and all ye need to know.

REFERENCES AND NOTES

I.

p. 5. Mr M. H. Spielmann, v. "Shakespeare's Portraiture", *Studies in the First Folio*, Oxford, 1924. Pp. 9–12.

p. 6. the frontispiece. For further information about this the reader should consult Thos. Kay, *The Grafton Portrait of Shakespeare*, 1914.

p. 7. Dr John Smart, i.e. *Shakespeare: truth and tradition*, Arnold, 1928.

p. 9. Dr A. C. Bradley, i.e. "Keats" in *Oxford Lectures on Poetry*.

p. 11. Sidney Lee. It is remarkable that as a young man Lee was much interested in Shakespearian topicality; it was he who first noticed the parallel between Shylock and Lopez, cf. pp. 82–4.

p. 13. "his tragic life-story", the sub-title of Frank Harris's *The Man Shakespeare*.

II.

p. 23. a puritan writer in 1587, i.e. Stephen Gosson, *Schoole of Abuse*.

p. 37. Incertainty that once gave scope, etc., from "Melancholia" by Robert Bridges (*Shorter Poems*, 1931, p. 173).

III.

p. 40. *The Merry Wives of Stratford*, v. Smart, *op. cit.* p. 56.

p. 43. Shakespeare's lost years in London, the title of a book by A. Acheson, publ. 1920.

p. 45. I am as sorry...approves his art, v. *Kindheart's Dream*, ed. G. B. Harrison (Bodley Head Quartos), p. 6.

There have been attempts of late, etc. By Smart (v. note, p. 7) and Peter Alexander in *Shakespeare's "Henry VI" and "Richard III"*, Cambridge, 1929.

p. 46. Henslowe freely employed, etc., v. Chambers, *Eliz. Stage*, II, 170–81.

p. 60. Mr J. A. Fort, i.e. *The Two Dated Sonnets of Shakespeare*, Oxford, 1924, and *A Time-scheme for Shakespeare's Sonnets*, Mitre Press, 1929; cf. also "The Mortal Moon" by G. B. Harrison, *Times Lit. Sup.* Nov. 29, 1928.

p. 65. *Love's Labour's Lost*, v. Introd. to ed. of the play in "The New Shakespeare".

IV.

p. 72. Ease and relaxation are profitable, etc., v. *Discoveries*, ed. by G. B. Harrison (Bodley Head Quartos), pp. 34–5.

p. 73. He was "the more to be admired", etc., v. Chambers, *Will. Shak.* II, 252.

p. 76. "negative capability", v. Keats, *Letters*, Dec. 22, 1817. The whole passage is of first-class importance.

p. 82. a certain Dr Lopez: cf. "Note on the Copy", *Merchant of Venice* (New Shakespeare).

p. 83. a wolf "hanged for human slaughter", v. *Merchant*, 4. 1. 130–37.

p. 84. inappropriately addressed to a Jew. I am aware that the petitions of the Lord's Prayer were based upon earlier Hebrew prayers; but Shakespeare was not a modern Biblical scholar and could not know this.

"grow guilty...outward part": *L. L. L.* 4. 1. 30–33.

p. 87. a passage in Rupert Brooke's *Memoir*, p. liii.

p. 91. *Twelfth Night*...the earliest recorded performance. On Feb. 2, 1602. In the ed. of the play in "The New Shakespeare", I was inclined to accept this as the date of composition; I now feel with Sir Edmund Chambers that "it is so akin in style and temper to *As You Like It* that a somewhat earlier date seems probable", e.g. the winter 1600–1 (v. Chambers, *Will. Shak.* I, 405).

V.

p. 96. "the centre and focus...in Europe", v. Chambers, *Shakespeare: a Survey*, pp. 140–1.

became a reformed character, v. W. B. Devereux, *Lives and Letters of the Earls of Essex*, I, 405.

Fluellen...Sir Roger Williams, v. present writer's *Martin Marprelate and Shakespeare's Fluellen*, Moring, 1912 (repr. from *The Library*).

p. 101. Dr Harrison...the theory, v. *Times Lit. Sup.* Nov. 20, 1930, "Shakespeare's Topical Significances".

p. 102. Elizabeth...compared with Richard II, v. Chambers, *Will. Shak.* II, 326–7.

p. 104. a reference to *Hamlet* in 1598 or soon after. Cf. G. Harvey's *Marginalia*, ed. G. C. Moore-Smith, pp. viii–xii.

Polonius...Burleigh. Cf. Chambers, *Will. Shak.* I, 418.

the Quarrel of the Theatres, v. Chambers, *Will. Shak.* I, 71; cf. below, pp. 110–11.

p. 106. prayer of Essex on the scaffold, v. Devereux, *op. cit.* II, 189.

p. 107. more in *Hamlet* than this. I am preparing a book on the dramatic problems of *Hamlet* in which the Essex business will play a very small part.

From 1601 to 1603 he writes nothing, E. K. Chambers places both *Merry Wives* (this "with some hesitation") and *Troilus* between *Hamlet* and *All's Well*, but his reasons for doing so seem to me weak. The break is partly explained by the death of Elizabeth and a severe outbreak of plague; but neither took effect until 1603. There was no plague 1601–2. The chronology of the plays is very difficult at this point; but, everything considered, 1603 or early 1604 seems the best date for *All's Well*.

VI.

p. 111. *The Merchant*...took the fancy of James I. The play, performed before him on Shrovesunday, 1605, was "againe commanded by the Kings Majestie" two days later; v. Chambers, *Will. Shak.* II, 332.

p. 113. failure to finish *Timon*. Cf. Chambers, *Will. Shak.* I, 482.

VII.

p. 129. Sir Edmund Chambers, v. *Will. Shak.* I, 85–6; *A Survey*, 245–6, 273–85.

p. 131. *Cymbeline*...buried with Tennyson, cf. *Alfred, Lord Tennyson: a memoir. By his son.* Pp. 774–77.

p. 135. words...about Wordsworth, v. Introd. to *The Poetry of the Age of Wordsworth*, 1927.

p. 136. These beauteous forms, etc. That Wordsworth is here writing not of the Lakes but of the Wye valley does not weaken the force of my argument.